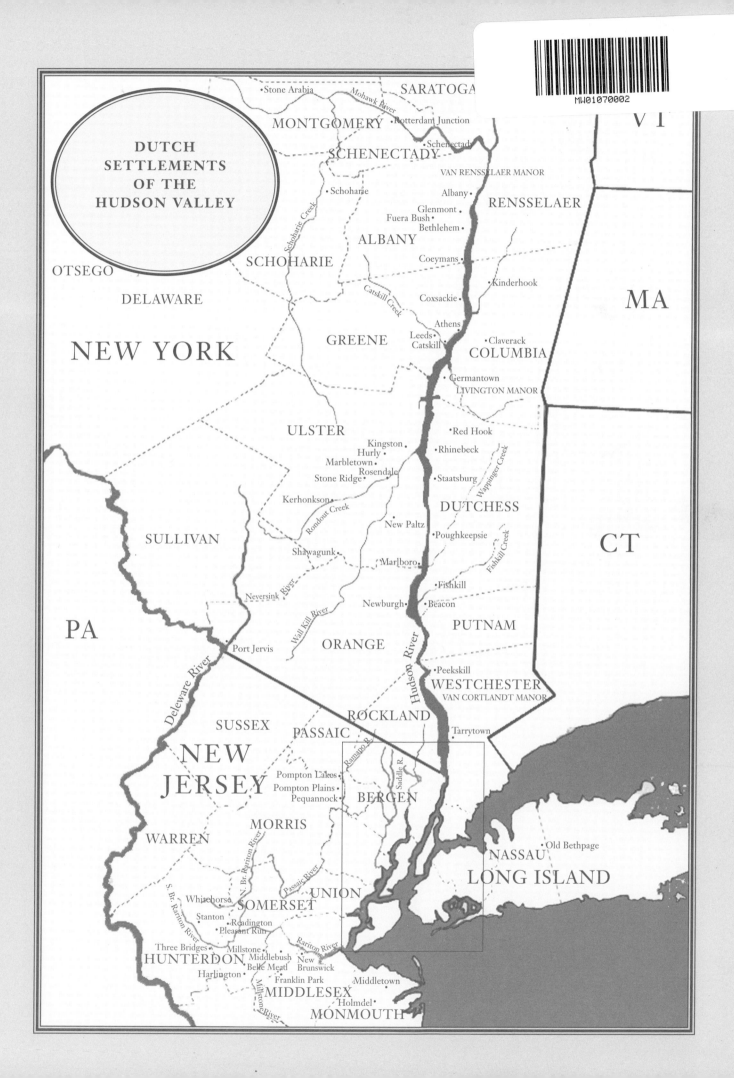

DUTCH SETTLEMENTS OF THE HUDSON VALLEY

NEW YORK

OTSEGO

DELAWARE

SARATOGA

MONTGOMERY
•Stone Arabia

Mohawk River

•Rotterdam Junction

SCHENECTADY
•Schenectady

•Schoharie

SCHOHARIE

Schoharie Creek

Catskill Creek

GREENE

VAN RENSSELAER MANOR

Albany•
Glenmont•
Fuera Bush•
Bethlehem•

ALBANY

RENSSELAER

Coeymans•

•Kinderhook

Coxsackie•

Athens•
Leeds•
Catskill•

COLUMBIA
•Claverack

•Germantown
LIVINGTON MANOR

MA

ULSTER

Kingston•
Hurly•
Marbletown•
Rosendale•
Stone Ridge•

•Red Hook

•Rhinebeck

Wappinger Creek

•Staatsburg

DUTCHESS

Kerhonkson•

Rondout Creek

•New Paltz

•Poughkeepsie

Fishkill Creek

CT

SULLIVAN

Shawagunk•

Neversink River

Wall Kill River

•Marlboro

•Fishkill

Newburgh•

•Beacon

Hudson River

ORANGE

PUTNAM

Deleware River

Port Jervis•

•Peekskill

WESTCHESTER
VAN CORTLANDT MANOR

PA

ROCKLAND

•Tarrytown

SUSSEX

PASSAIC

Ramapo R.

Saddle R.

NEW JERSEY

Pompton Lakes•
Pompton Plains•
Pequannock•

BERGEN

MORRIS

WARREN

N. Br. Rariton River

Passaic River

NASSAU
•Old Bethpage

LONG ISLAND

S. Br. Rariton River

Whitehorse•

SOMERSET
Stanton•
•Readington
•Pleasant Run

UNION

Three Bridges•
Millstone•
Middlebush•
Belle Meatl•

Rariton River

New•
Brunswick•

HUNTERDON
Harlington•

Franklin Park•

•Middletown

Millstone River

MIDDLESEX
Holmdel•

MONMOUTH

VT

Dutch Colonial Homes
in America

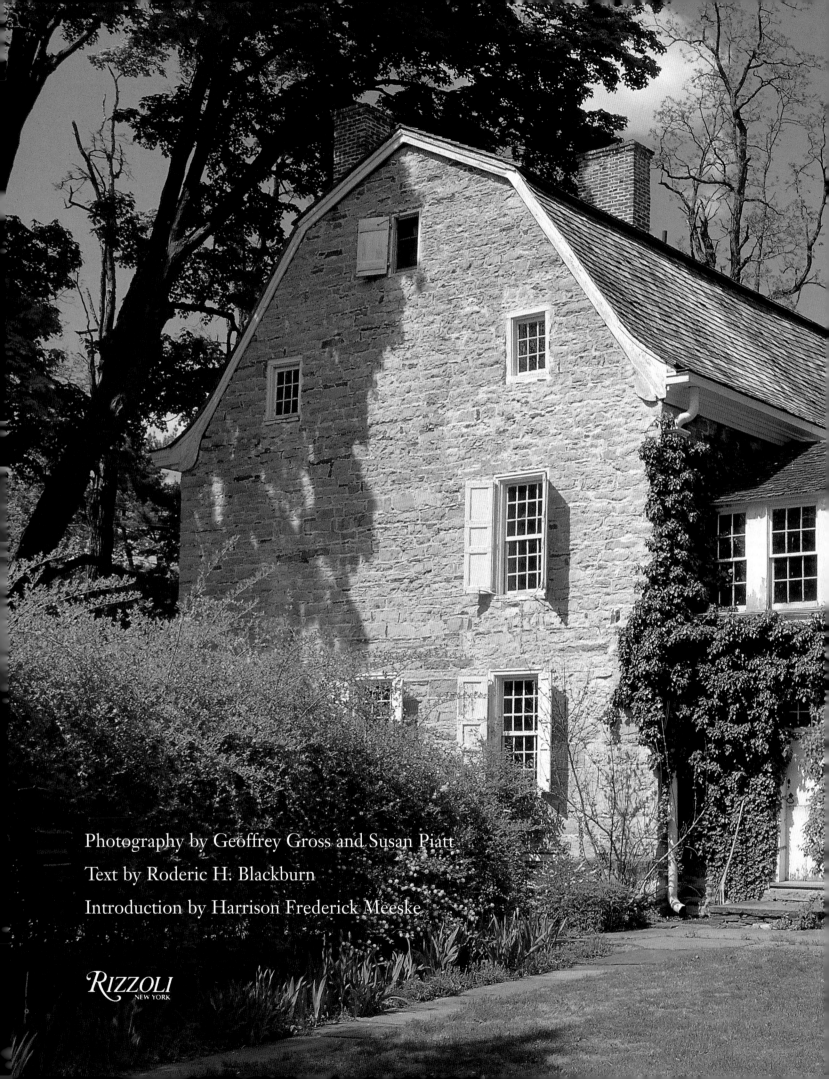

Photography by Geoffrey Gross and Susan Piatt

Text by Roderic H. Blackburn

Introduction by Harrison Frederick Meeske

RIZZOLI
NEW YORK

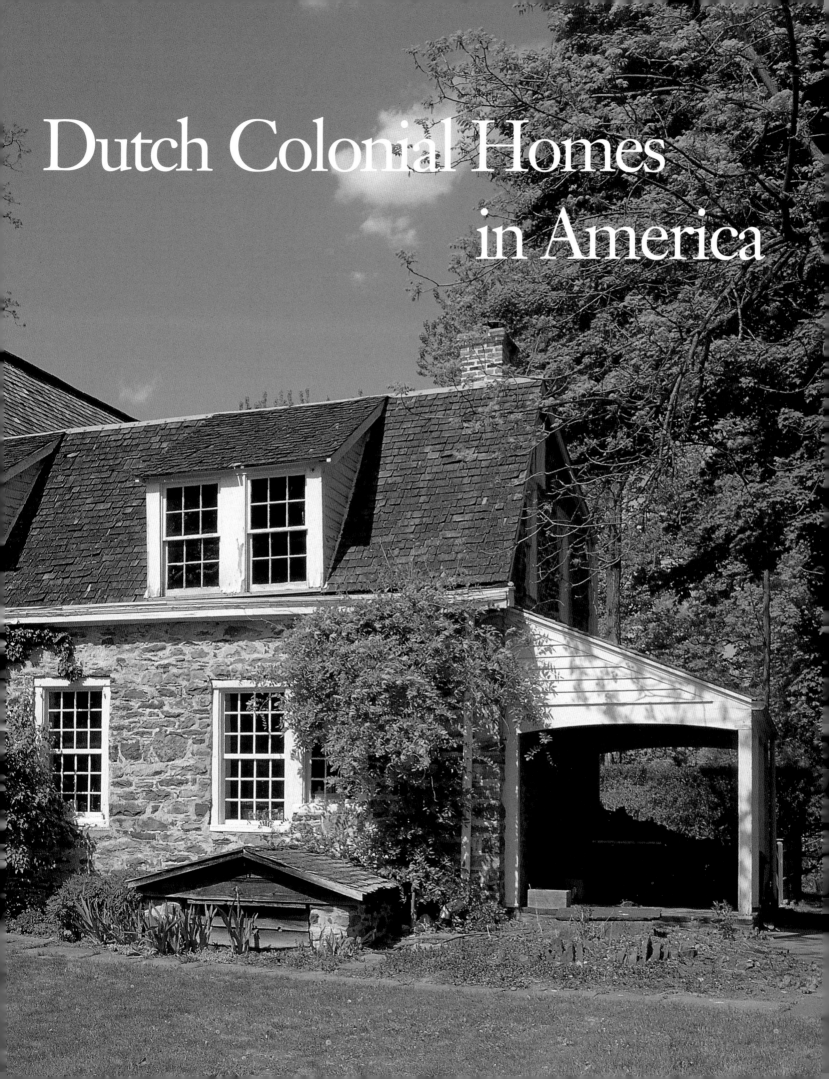

Dutch Colonial Homes
in America

First published in the United States of America in 2002 by
RIZZOLI INTERNATIONAL PUBLICATIONS, INC.
300 Park Avenue South, New York, NY 10010

ISBN: 0-8478-2466-7
Library of Congress Control Number: 2002102947

Designed by Abigail Sturges
Project Editor: Kristen Schilo

Distributed to the United States trade by St. Martin's Press

Printed and bound in China

Cover: Van Alen House (pp. 62-67)
Back cover: Garden, Schermerhorn House (pp. 68-71)
Endpapers: Maps by Lindsey Farrell
Half title page: Wynkoop House (pp. 154-163)
Title page: Wynkoop House (pp. 154-163)
Pages 4, 5: Burgis view of New York City, 1721, detail
Page 6: Delft tiles from parlor fireplace of De Klerck House (pp. 168-171)

This publication is supported in part by grants from:
Furthermore, the publication program of the J.M. Kaplan Fund
The Holland Society
The New York Council for the Humanities
The National Endowment for the Humanities
The New York Foundation for the Arts
The Netherland-America Foundation
The Society of the Daughters of Holland Dames
Mr. and Mrs. Mark S. Gross
Van Voorhees Family Association
Bob and Stacy Schmetterer
Lorraine Lombardi

2002 2003 2004 2005 2006 / 10 9 8 7 6 5 4 3 2 1

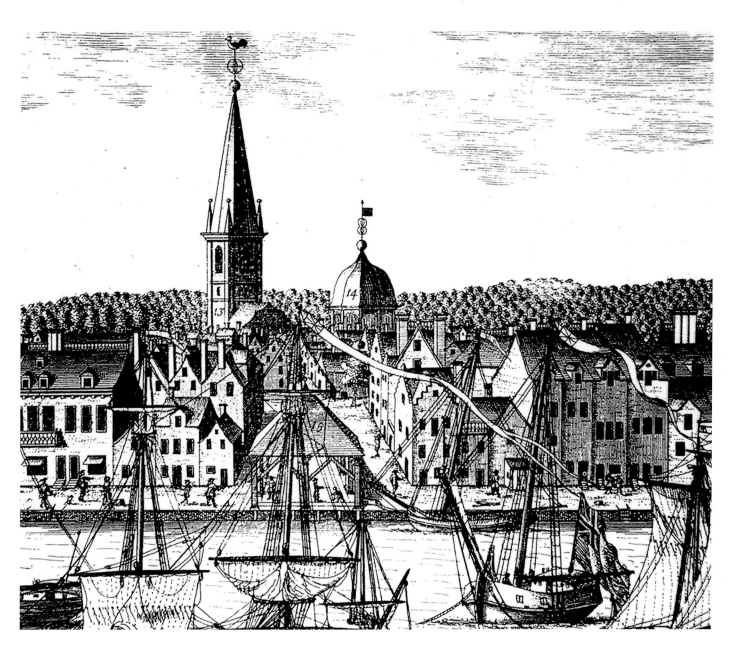

*To my parents, Joan and Mark;
and for Alice, my little girl.* —G.G.

*To my parents Evelyn and Raymond who taught
me the love of history and architecture.* —S.P.

To the muse of Cornelis Schermerhorn. —R.H.B.

Contents

Preface

Roderic H. Blackburn

One day in 1998, Geoffrey Gross stopped by my office in Kinderhook, New York, having seen my publications on Dutch culture, and told me about his desire to do a book on Dutch houses in New York and New Jersey. He showed me a portfolio of photos on various subjects that he had taken over the years. They were exceptionally beautiful. I immediately proposed that we collaborate on an article I was doing for *The Magazine Antiques* about a Connecticut house. I introduced him to Hank Meeske who was also working on a book on Dutch houses for which I was writing the introduction and then gave him a list of houses and their owners. The result is a book which has now come to fruition, conceived by Geoffrey Gross and Susan Piatt, for which I have contributed the text, and Harrison Meeske the introduction. The qualities that inspired Geoffrey's love for Dutch houses are evident in every photograph. Readers cannot but be moved by what he has captured on film. Indeed the purpose of this book is just that, to visually inspire others through close personal exposure to a fascinating culture now present only in its remnants.

Compared to other colonial regions little has been said about the Dutch in text books, architectural treatises, and the media, and there are many misconceptions and stereotypes that have been perpetuated therein. Cultural codes underlie the one non-English society that founded a colony among the original thirteen. Dutch cultural codes are the fundamental principles on which their society and beliefs—and what they built—were founded. These codes are best learned in the fatherland where an unbroken continuity of life continues to this day.

Both Hank and I have had the pleasure of doing research in The Netherlands. As the reader will observe, explaining how and why the Dutch built their structures as they did involves several levels of analysis. First is an account of the creation, settlement, and development of New Netherland, the Dutch colony, and then of the Dutch under the English who acquired the colony in 1664 but left the Dutch to their own ways. I mention the cultural beliefs the Dutch brought to the New World that affected how they lived and what they lived for. A short discussion follows about the Dutch (and English) social system, government, church, family, and business by which people were organized to pursue their goals. This is followed by an account of the origin of house design and function in The Netherlands and its introduction into America, with a comparison to the medieval house-building concepts of the English, Germans, and Swedes, showing how their ideas were partially adopted by the Dutch. The evolution of the Dutch house is then described structurally in terms of changes in features, materials, furnishings, and room arrangements. These are explained functionally, showing how structural changes in rooms affected all other features of a house, especially fireplace type, chimney placement, roof shape, and the use of the second story. Human needs for warmth and cooling, privacy, convenience, and comfort are shown to be major influences on house evolution. Based on these precepts, a functional technique for interpreting the house is proposed by which houses can be "read" to discover changes and their causes.

The photographs are divided into sections corresponding to three geo-cultural regions. Each of these regions has certain features of geography, natural resources, and Dutch settlement, history, and architecture that distinguishes it from the others. From north to south in New York state, these geo-cultural regions include the upper Hudson and Mohawk River Valleys (basically colonial Albany County); the mid- and lower Hudson River Valley (Ulster, Dutchess, Putnam, Westchester, and Orange Counties); and western Long Island which shares much with the counties of New Jersey, and even Rockland County in New York. Each section is introduced by a discussion of these regional features and why houses in each are different from those in the other regions.

What this book does not cover, since it is defined by photographs of existing buildings associated with Dutch style architecture and Dutch owned structures, are buildings which no longer exist. You will not see here Dutch houses in Manhattan, Albany, Schenectady, and New Brunswick where a distinctive Netherlands style of urban house once existed but is now entirely gone or so altered as to be nearly indistinguishable.

Previous page: Great Room, The Cornelis Schermerhorn House, Kinderhook, NY.

Frame and shutter, Van Zandt House, Albany, NY.

The selection of houses and other structures that are included in the book came about because of the purposes of the book, as previously stated. We were looking for a number of features and qualities including houses, or parts, that retained untouched original surfaces. Some detail images show pieces of a wall, parts of a molding, a latch, or scratches on a window. Other images have visual excitement such as the sweeping shape of a roof, the pattern of Dutch bond bricks, or the cast of light on a bare wall. These evoke for us a sense of the aesthetics that the Dutch brought to their own building ideas. Also illustrated is the range and variation of existing house and barn types to show structural change over time in style and over regions in form and materials.

Some houses are restorations with period furnishings—mostly house museums—purporting to reflect how the Dutch lived. Other images are of houses inhabited today and that are fur-

nished according to taste—some with antiques, others with the comforts of modern life. We did not seek to emphasize period settings because there are relatively few of these, but also we have concluded that even the best are only a partial reflection of what they may have been like in their own time.

This book takes a more anthropological than historical approach. I seek to explain behavior more than events and to do that I look for the underlying needs, beliefs, and values that characterize an ethnic group like the Dutch and motivate their behavior. When it comes to explaining why the Dutch built houses in the way they did and lived in them in distinctive ways, the number of influencing factors—geographic, economic, social, cultural, and so on—are great and complex.

This is a book about the Dutch and their architecture, but exactly who were the Dutch? Today we know that the Dutch are the citizens of The Netherlands, a nation more commonly if erroneously called Holland (which is the name of two of its several provinces—North and South Holland.) But in 1609, when the first Dutchmen laid eyes on what is now the Hudson River, The Netherlands was just a collection of ethnically diverse provinces beginning to form a state independent of Spanish control, called the United Provinces. When immigrants began arriving in New Netherland, starting in 1624, upward of half had not been born and raised in the United Provinces—they came from other regions such as the nearby German states, Flanders (now Belgium), Denmark, Norway, and France. So when we speak of the Dutch of this region in the seventeenth and eighteenth centuries we are referring to a heterogeneous group of people, half of whose immigrant ancestors did not come from The Netherlands but shared some common beliefs, language, and identity either because they came from a common cultural area in Europe (sharing many common traits that extended from Denmark southerly along th North Sea coast through present day Netherlands and Belgium all the way to Normandy in France) or assimilated into the predominant Dutch culture in the New World. They "became Dutch" just as the Dutch, ironically, were becoming acculturated to the politically dominant English society after 1664.

Foreword

Geoffrey Gross

Through photography I have discovered a complex, emotionally rich, multi-level culture—the Dutch of colonial America who were, in a surprising number of ways, similar to our own society. In a sense they predicted, not just preceded, contemporary America. With the camera I have sought to reveal this truth.

The camera does more than record a likeness or image of the past. It reveals—as Edward Weston has said—*thingness*, that which an object is, its own presence in the world. It has a reality wholly separate and independent from the perceptions of others who see with their own preconceptions. The subject exists independently on its own and should be perceived as an individual entity endowed with a "beingness" unique to it.

This concept goes back to Jan Van Eyck, the fifteenth-century Flemish painter whose work prefigured the Enlightenment's focus on the secular. He revolutionized painting by depicting common objects and people of the bourgeoisie. His choice of non-religious subject matter coupled with his use of color and texture—painting for the sake of painting—allied his art closely with the emerging concept of the individual. In effect, he made art as integral to life as food, shelter, clothing, and the home.

Nearly two centuries later we find Van Eyck's legacy alive in The Netherlands. Paintings from their "Golden Age" capture, preserve, and extol everyday life in all aspects—the sacred along with the profane—expressing the aspirations and needs of all levels of Dutch society. These images of life, produced by the greatest image makers of their day (who readily accepted and incorporated whatever technical means available) convey to us a society and culture much like our own. For this reason it is intriguing to use similar technology to rediscover and understand them and, in so doing, to understand ourselves as well.

Photography allows for the preservation and presentation of time and space. The basic tools of modern-day photography—light, color, texture, time, and space—if handled

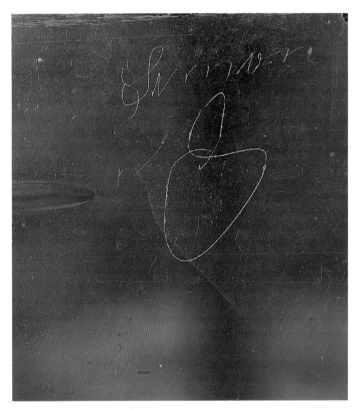

Window pane, The Mabee Farm, Rotterdam Junction, NY.

and mixed effectively, speak to us in a visual language quite unique to the camera. By careful manipulation it is possible to present and preserve moments, objects, places, and emotions which otherwise would be lost forever, and never experienced or even contemplated. Very often these images present that which is most familiar to us in a totally new way or "new light," as if never seen before. A photograph of a door knocker, for example, a basic utilitarian object handled by many people in the course of a single day, can become, through sensitive photo-interpretation, so much more than an inconsequential daily tool.

It depends not just on what you see but how you look if you are to truly discover what has not been obvious. The camera lends to each person a new set of eyes, enabling, even commanding, us to look again—to see anew. Those who view this book and who have never encountered Dutch houses will have their eyes opened to an entirely new experience. Those who have known Dutch houses and barns will find that even those sites, although familiar, appear quite differently from their own visual memory. It has only required the camera (and camerman), with its special and unique abilities, to reacquaint us with our own beginnings, now seen in a new way.

Working Method

In its basic form, the camera is nothing more than a light-tight enclosure with a small opening on one side to admit light and a surface opposite this opening for the image to appear on. This image may then be traced, or otherwise recorded. Today we capture this image through chemicals or with electronic sensors. Through experience, the operator of the *camera obscura* quickly learned to manipulate the apparatus to produce a visually pleasing, well-ordered view of the home and environs. Succinct compositions with "squared-up lines" resulted.

Modern-day scholars, historians, and physicists have reconstructed rooms resembling scenes from old paintings. They have employed computers and mathematical formulas to prove the use of the *camera obscura* by the "Old Masters." Yet all that was really necessary was to find a well-seasoned interior photographer. Anyone who has spent the better part of a lifetime looking through an 8 x 10 camera can readily attest to the utilization of the *camera obscura*. In fact, there are paintings extant today where the painter was so true to the reality presented by the lens that linear distortion introduced by this method was depicted in the painting.

There are other reasons why you may see similarities between the pictures in this book and those in Dutch seventeenth-century paintings. Before the appearance of electric light, life was quite different. During the day, and whenever possible, all activities were carried out either outdoors or, if indoors, quite close to a window. Candles were an extravagance and used sparingly. It is no accident that early paintings of Dutch interiors appear so appealing when illuminated by candlelight. They were never intended to be illuminated to the extent that modern living requires. Where possible, I have attempted to recreate this interior glow, while at the same time illuminating the interiors well enough to allow a glimpse into the life of the former inhabitants. This appearance of "available light" in many photographs is, in fact, the result of the careful mixing of artificial illumination with existing or ambient light in a manner which will fully present the interior and allow the viewer to enter.

Another similarity between the old paintings and new photographs of Dutch life is our shared perspective on the "common man" and his way of life. William Morris, the great proponent of the Arts and Crafts movement of the nineteenth century, thought that technology wrought by the Industrial Revolution had become a great evil. He and other compatriots attempted to revive handicrafts, the guild system, and other aspects of medieval times which he believed were much more in tune with the human spirit. Perhaps this is also why we share a love for Dutch paintings as both cultures shared a similar sensibility for the individual and his experiences. We need only to look at the pre-industrial Netherlands of the mid-seventeenth century to see that art was everywhere, closely integrated into the fabric of daily life: Farmers went to market and purchased art to adorn their modest homes. Thus we find that this culture, which at first glance seems so remote to us today, is actually within us. We need only to make the small effort to realize and appreciate our own past and thus to inform ourselves of our real place in the present. Without a clear understanding of our past we cannot enter a better future.

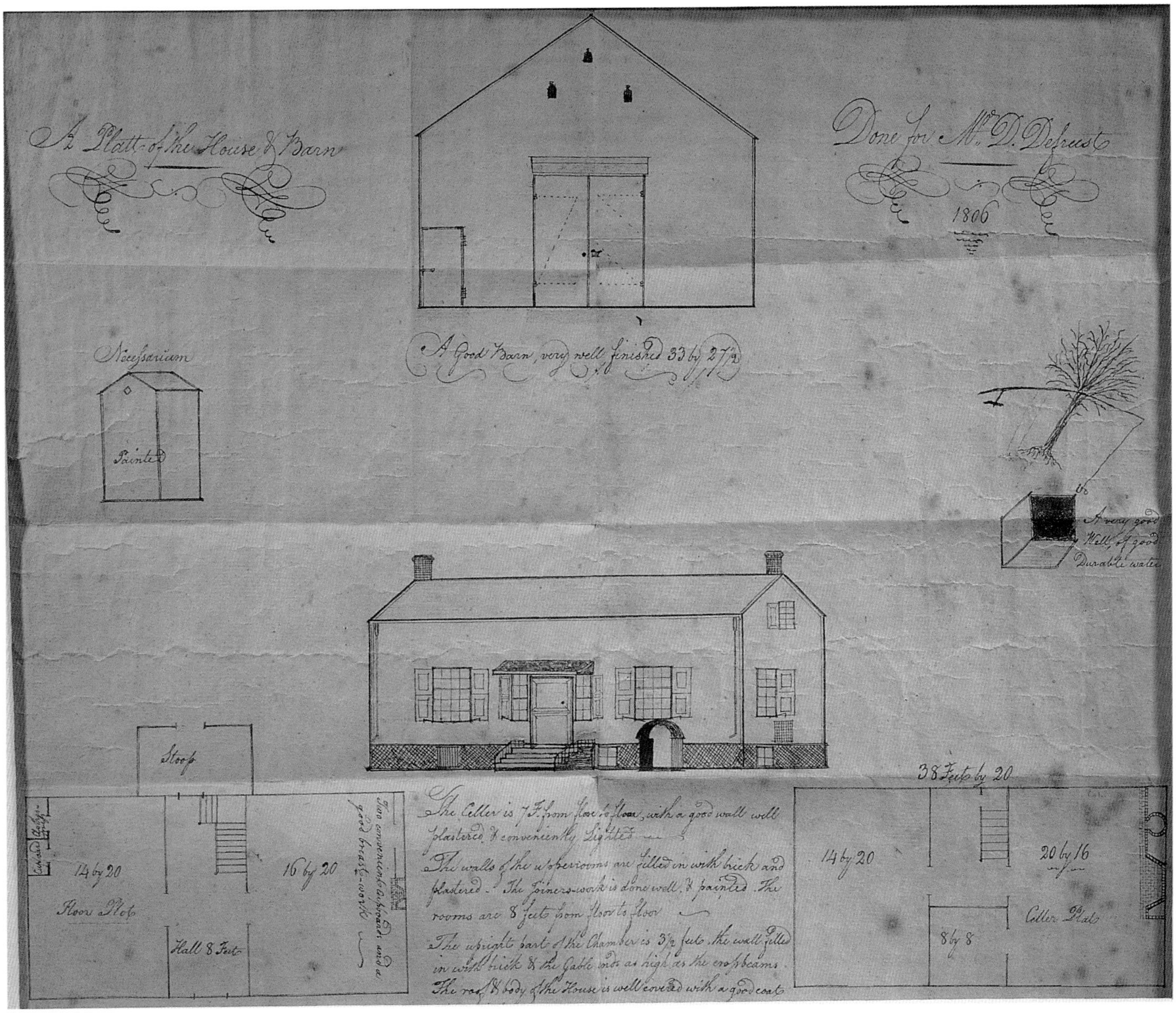
A Platt of the House & Barn
Done for Mr. D. Defreest
1806
A Good Barn, very well finished 33 by 27½
Necessarium
Painted
A very good Well of good Durable water
Stoop
14 by 20
16 by 20
Floor Plot
Hall 8 Feet
The Celler is 7 F. from floor to floor, with a good wall well plastered, & conveniently Lighted
The walls of the upper rooms are filled in with brick and plastered. The Joiners-work is done well, & painted. The rooms are 8 feet from floor to floor
The upright part of the Chamber is 3½ feet, the wall filled in with brick & the Gable ends as high as the cross beams
The roof & body of the House is well covered with a good coat
38 Feets by 20
14 by 20
20 by 16
8 by 8
Celler Plot

David de Freest Farm
Rensselaer County, New York
Eastfield Village, East Nassau, New York

This remarkable hand-drawn document appears to serve as a descriptive advertisement for a late Dutch/Early Federal "Platt of the house and barn . . . Done for Mr. D. Defreest 1806." It describes a center hall house of a story-and-a-half, twenty by thirty-eight feet, with a stoop, brick-filled walls, a "Necessarium, Painted" (outhouse), a well with "Durable water," and a "Good Dutch barn, very well finished 33 by 27½." The house would appear to date from about 1780–90, but in this conservative region others like it date as late as the 1806 of this plan.

On the 10 Day of December in the Year of our Lord 1719 Was I Desired by one Johannis Appel To Survey his Land Called Onnisquatha Situate Lying And being in the County of Albany on the South Side there of And he the Said Johannis Appel Desired Me the Same Time to peruse his Title Which he had for the Said Land In the first Place he shewed Me A Pattaint under the Great Seal of This Province of New York Bearing Date the 30th Day of March 1685 which Pattaint I Perused and found that it was not only for the Land Particuler therein Mentioned, but A Confirmation of an Indian Purchas Which Tunis Slingerlant and the Said Johannis Appel hath Made at the City Hall of Albany on the 8 Day of May 1685, which Said Purchas I found was made by Virtue Of a Licence from This Province Bearing Date the 6 day of March 1684⅗ The Said Pattaint Says that it may More full and at Large appear by the Said Purchas And found that the Purchas Made Mention of Mark with Tree For his the Said Johannis Appels Bound So that I Desired him the Said Joh: Appell if he could Show me this Tree by Creditable Christians Witness And not by Indians. Which he accordingly did And thereupon I have Surveyed this Land Onnisquatha by the Information of the Witness and Showed me the Markith Tree; It begins at a Certain Marsh or Meddow on the North End thereof by a Tree Markith with the Baer Wolf and Turtill from thence South 85 Deg: East 15 Chains to a Tree Marked With ditto Marks Thence South 45 Deg: East 170 Chains to a Tree With Ditto Marks And Stands on the Side of the Road Which leads from Onnisquatha to Normans Kill Thence South 50 Deg: East 132 Chains to an other Tree with Ditto Marks And Stands on the Side of the Road Which leads from Onnisquatha to Albany thence South 10 Deg: East 228 Chains to another Tree with Ditto Marks And Stands on the Side of a Run of Water Called Kley Kill thence South 55 Deg: East 25 Chains to Another Tree with ditto Marks which Stands about 5 Chains over the great Onnisquatha Kill thence South 68 Deg: West 158 Chains to Another Tree with ditto Marks And Stands on the Side of the Road which leads from Onnisquatha to Haghelock thence North 42 Deg: West 50 Chains to Another Tree with Ditto Marks thence North 65 Deg: West 44 Chains to an other tree With Ditto Marks And Stands on the Side of the Clyn Onnisquathas Kill thence North 68 Deg: West 146 Chains to another Tree With Ditto Marks and Stands on the North End of a Lake or Inwater thence North 55 Deg: West 142 Chains to Another Tree Stands on the Side of foot path Which leads to Schohare and on the Side of the great Onnisquatha Kill Thence North 55 Deg: East 192 Chains to the place Where first begun the Same Containing in 9874 Acres the Same Surveyed By Me the Day and Year above Written

Nicholas Schuyler Surveyor

Introduction

Harrison Frederick Meeske

A quick perusal through the following pages of photographs will reveal a dark truth: houses identified as Dutch Colonial vary significantly from one another depending on when and in what region they were built.

There are several hundred, perhaps over a thousand Dutch Colonial houses surviving. They were erected beginning in the mid-seventeenth century up until the outbreak of the Revolution in 1776. A survey of surviving Dutch Colonial houses—conducted by Helen Wilkinson Reynolds in the late nineteen twenties—clearly demonstrated these regional and time-specific attributes which reflected adaptations over the years to the evolving needs and perceptions of the occupants, as well as changes in fashion and available technology.

The Dutch had experience farming rich bottomlands; much of The Netherlands was reclaimed from the sea. By choice, therefore, most Dutch settlers built homes in riparian low-lands within yards of navigable water; they herded cattle and sheep on coastal salt-grass meadows or on the necks and islands of rivers. By occupying the riparian lowlands the Dutch engendered the envy of their Yankee neighbors stuck with the hardscrabble rocky heights throughout much of New England. Eventually the rich bottom lands of the Hudson Valley attracted Yankee immigrants, competition, and eventual annexation of the Dutch settlements by the English.

The riverine pattern of settlement expedited the traffic in people and cargo at a time when the overland transport of bulk goods was physically daunting. Dozens of sloops plied the Hudson River and the adjacent coastal waters. Many Dutch traders ventured as far as the Caribbean with wheat and other produce of Dutch farms in the Hudson Valley. On return trips upriver they supplied farmers and merchants with finished products imported from overseas or made in New York or other coastal cities.

The main material imported for house building was glass, which was expensive; early houses usually had only a few small glazed windows. Almost every other building material was made or obtained locally. Timber for joists and boards was felled and hewn locally, often adjacent to the building site, and pre-assembled by housewrights within yards of where the house was to be raised. Bricks, and in some areas pantiles for roofing, were burnt locally from the clay that was common throughout much of the Hudson Valley. Where stone, especially stratified limestone and sandstone, was available it became the preferred building material as it was cheaper and required fewer masonry skills than brick, and was more durable and stylish than wooden clapboards. As in all colonial architecture site-specific timber, stone, and clay were primarily selected on the basis of economic factors. In contemporary times, the aesthetic importance of employing local materials was recognized as an important consideration in unifying a structure and its location.

If we look at each region the relationship between local building materials and styles becomes more obvious. The houses are distinctive in design by the date of construction and often regionally specific within the wide territory claimed by the Dutch—an area that encompassed the Delaware to the Connecticut River Valleys and Staten Island inland up the Hudson River to the Mohawk River Valley. With the passage of time, regional variations in houses developed among the Dutch homesteaders reflecting the local diversity of readily available resources. In the near absence of stratified rock or clay, Dutch Colonial houses on Long Island were usually built of wood. Stylistically this lent itself to creating over-hanging "Flemish"-style spring eaves. New Jersey houses were frequently built of squared local brownstone with wide low-pitch bell-shaped gambrel roofs. Although stone was rarely used in The Netherlands it became the traditional building material in several sections of the Hudson Valley at an early date. Ulster County houses were almost all made of limestone with pitched roofs, whereas across the Hudson River in Dutchess County, fieldstone houses were frequently built with brick gables and gambrel roofs.

In the north, in Rensselaerwyck and Fort Orange, which later became Albany County under the English (today it encompasses several counties), the brick house was popular among the more prosperous farmers. Using a traditional

Netherlands material also resulted in copying most closely the traditional Netherlands style. Houses were built with "spout" gables and steep pitched roofs. A few still survive from Kinderhook to Schenectady. By the 1760s, brick houses with high-breaking gambrel roofs were built in this area as English taste came to predominate.

The earliest homes usually had one room and were one-and-a-half floors in height; by contrast, early English Colonial houses often had rooms on two floors. Larger Dutch houses had two or even three ground-floor rooms joined at the gables, sometimes with a separate outside entry to each room. The buildings were one-room deep and, with the exception of a few side aisle buildings, typically had no hall or passageway connecting the various chambers. The ground floor of a Dutch house was dedicated to residential uses; the upper half story was primarily used for storage of grain and other items, as a place to weave, and as a sleeping area for older children, hired hands, or slaves.

A fundamental difference exists in the construction and function of Dutch and English chimney and fireplace design. The Dutch fireplace design, common in Dutch homes until the mid-eighteenth century, consisted of a hearth supported by an arched masonry base in the cellar—it looks somewhat like a flueless fireplace—or by a cradle of wooden members containing rocks and masonry, directly beneath the hearth stones. The fireplace had a masonry rear wall but opened into the room without "jambs" or walls at the sides. The chimney rested on a beam above the hearth of a Dutch fireplace and a wide brick flue lead to a smoke chamber in the garret before exiting via a light brickwork chimney. The early English design called for a massive central masonry base supporting several flues and hearths; the chimney also functioned as a central support for the frame beams of the house.

Early Dutch rooms were usually plastered, the wooden structural frame members and the wooden planked ceilings were left exposed; Anglo-American rooms were frequently paneled with boards or planks and at an early date the ceiling beams were concealed and plastered over. In the mid-eighteenth

century English fashions prevailed and Anglo-Dutch rooms were often fitted with paneling and the ceiling beams and planking were covered with lathe and then plastered.

Within Dutch houses were a number of culturally specific Netherlander features. The principal cultural markers include Dutch jambless hearths, commonly built until the mid-eighteenth century in the conservative upper Hudson Valley. They were replaced at that time by more efficient English-style fireplaces; elsewhere they were converted earlier. If it was affordable, many Dutch homeowners also elected to decorate their hearths with Delft tiles that had illustrations drawn from nature, folk culture, or the Bible. In addition, there were enclosed stairways to grain-storage garrets and gable doors with hoist mechanisms to lift heavy articles to the garret lofts. The divided door with flanking benches, commonly called a Dutch door, was built at an entry's front steps, still called stoops in New York. These were important and ubiquitous features found on the colonial houses of Anglo-Dutch people.

Houses were filled with typically Dutch furnishings that included large storage cabinets called *kasten* (*kast* or *kas*, singular) for linen and valuables. Other pieces were the *pottebanks*, or open-dish shelving that once graced kitchens, as well as distinctive fiddleback chairs, gate-leg tables, and various Delft articles, both utilitarian and decorative.

Dutch Colonial architecture is based upon a Netherlands concept that dates back to the Middle Ages. The one fundamental and distinctive feature that by itself identifies a house as truly Dutch is the anchor-bent or H-bent frame. An anchor-bent or H-bent frame looks like a football goal post. It is an H-shaped unit consisting of two vertical, squared members or posts joined by a squared horizontal member or beam set and joined several feet below the top of the posts. Each H-bent is a distinct framing unit that anchors the structure of the house. In early houses the anchor-bent beam was buttressed by angled braces called corbels seated into the posts below the joint. Anchor-bent construction absolutely separates a Dutch house from the typical Anglo-American box-frame houses of New England

and the southern colonies. While the English box frame consists of two pre-assembled eave-wall sub-assemblies that were raised and connected by tie beams, the Dutch builder raised a series of individual H-bent units that were then joined on the eave walls—at the base by sills and at the top by plates. The roof structure consisted of a series of rafters joined in pairs at their apex; the rafter pairs were connected a few feet below their apex by a wind brace. The roof did not require a unifying roof-tree beam connecting the pairs of rafters to each other but was frequently planked over before being shingled.

Dutch barns are framed in the same H-bent system, only the timber members are larger in scale. Barns were three-aisles wide, while houses were most often one-aisle wide; an aisle being defined as the space between the anchor-bent posts for a house and the space between the posts and an aisle on the outside of each set of posts in a barn. Dutch barns were primarily used for storing grain so the loft and center aisle were dedicated to threshing and storage; the two side aisles sheltered livestock.

In both Dutch houses and barns all structural elements were visible and essential parts of the aesthetic of the house. In the houses, structural members of the H-bent were planed smooth and the anchor-bent beams frequently finished with a decorative beveled edge. The anchor-bent beams were planked over to serve as the attic floor above, while below they were exposed to serve as the ceiling of the first-floor room; the floor functioned as the cellar ceiling. Both garret-floor and cellar-ceiling surfaces were less carefully finished than exposed surfaces within the main floor unless the garret and/or cellar were used for living spaces. When the English Georgian fashion for plaster ceilings became the vogue the beams were covered; these beams may therefore be smooth, but rough beams were never intended to be exposed. Most Dutch Colonial houses used below-grade areas for storage and as root cellars, however cellars frequently served as a kitchen area. Below-grade-level kitchens are more commonly found when a house was built on a slope and the cellar opened at ground level at one side.

In houses made with stone walls the posts of the H-bent were omitted; the beams are seated in niches left in the masonry, the stone walls acting as "bearing walls" of sufficient strength to support the beams. Massive wooden frames were employed for doors and windows built directly into the stonework. In all other respects stone houses followed the basic pattern of Dutch construction—square rooms, open fireplaces, finished beams, and flooring. Traditional Dutch brick houses, although of masonry, did not have strong bearing walls like stone houses. Brick houses have anchor-bent frames identical to wooden houses. The external layer of bricks is merely a non-supportive envelope that provides fire resistance, elegance, and insulation but is identical in function to clapboard siding. The more modest—and less expensive—clapboard houses' walls were insulated by filling them with baked or unbaked brick or a lathe and mud in-filling. Early Anglo-American buildings often have a woven mesh called "wattle" and loose clay called "dab" as the wall in-filling material which is not typical of early Dutch construction.

Interior walls were plastered and whitewashed. In the early period the smoothly finished Dutch anchor-bent members, ceilings, and floors were kept unpainted and they became smoother by periodic washing. Dutch floors were laid and spiked rather than pegged, the unfinished surface frequently scoured and strewn with clean sand. Only in the late eighteenth century did paint on beams become generally acceptable, however the houses were brightened with color from the beginning. Frames of windows and doors, fireplace mantles and pilasters, and the wall posts—if not corbels, beams, and flooring—were painted in the early colonial period. These painted elements stood out dramatically against the normally white lime-washed walls. The Dutch have traditionally exhibited their affection for strong colors and in the colonies they displayed their taste with conviction. Paints were made from ground pigments derived from natural sources such as minerals. These were mixed with linseed oil or milk (casein) and applied directly to the bare, unprimed wood. The most common colors were red (close to Venetian red), red-brown ("Spanish brown"), blue-gray (made from charcoal), and a vermilion made from the mineral red lead. White, yellow ochre, yellow, and green are also among the more common colors. The colors were used monochromatically or—especially on doors and shutters—in combination.

With few exceptions, colonial houses have been modified, modernized, and defaced in the name of progress: Dutch jambless fireplaces were converted to English-style fireplaces by the middle of the eighteenth century; early houses with leaded windows that had iron braces in distinctive Dutch-style frames were changed to sash windows in the middle of the eighteenth century; dormers, rare in original Dutch construction, were added; and first-floor gable end windows were added when paneled walls went out of fashion in the nineteenth century. Even roof lines were changed from pitch roofs to gambrels when some houses were deepened and the garret was divided into rooms. Then when some houses were raised to two full stories, gambrel roofs were changed back to single-pitched roofs.

Houses also expanded outward. As family size and wealth increased, the homesteaders' single-room dwellings were expanded to become series' of rooms joined latterly at the gables. Houses originally fitted with separate doors to the exterior from each room were revised to become center-hall dwellings and early homes built one-room deep were doubled in depth by the addition of a second row of rooms at the rear. Wings, ells, sheds, and entirely new houses were built onto, around, or over older buildings. The original house might end up as a kitchen at the rear or be torn down and lost entirely except for the foundation. As a result of these often undocumented changes deeds, titles, date stones, and traditions are garbled, confused, and sometimes purposely misrepresented. An old house requires detective work that is a challenge and therefore a joy or a frustration depending on successful "reading" of the evidence.

Clues to the past are seldom entirely erased and many mysteries may be unraveled with logic, experience, and an eye for details: a single extra-deep anchor beam provides a clue to the location of a long-gone jambless fireplace; a single corbel left in an otherwise later-style room indicates structural modernization at some time in the past; and stairways and upper-floor rooms indicate modernization and expansion to an early structure. Cellar walls and beams and fireplace foundations reveal evolutionary developments from the ground up. Frequently an old window or doorway will be discovered hidden within, under, or between later construction. Finished beams above a plaster ceiling indicate earlier exposure, and walls and wooden members of different thicknesses or varying types of lathe in adjacent walls are indicators of different periods of development.

Geoffrey Gross' photographs of a wide selection of authentic Dutch houses therefore serves as an important document providing clarification for an often confused and misrepresented genre. Many of the rooms photographed in this book are in private homes and reflect changes to accommodate modern life. Houses were lived in differently in the past. Before the mid-eighteenth century, few rooms were dedicated to specific functions beyond what we conceive as a kitchen and a parlor. Dining rooms, bedrooms, and living rooms are all post-Dutch Colonial features unknown to the original builders. Homesteads once humble are now grand. The Dutch farmer might have in his *groote kamer* (great or best room, or parlor) his curtained-in bed, while a child might sleep in a trundle bed pulled out from under the master's with a baby in a cradle beside the bed. In 1749 Peter Kalm remarked that, at least in Albany, some houses had beds "partitioned off," as was a common practice in The Netherlands. Sons might climb a ladder and sleep with the slaves in the garret among the wheat sacks or make do in a corner of the kitchen. A family lived closely in a two-room house—cooking, eating, working, and playing in a proximity that would amaze many latter-day occupants.

The gorgeous photography that Geoffrey Gross and Susan Piatt bring to the subject will inspire greater curiosity about Dutch Colonial architecture and culture. The images create a palpable sense of what it was like to live in these houses at the time they were built.

Hutch, The Daniel De Klerck House (later the John DeWint House)

Tappan, Rockland County, New York

The pottery shelf (*potte-bank* in Dutch) was a common feature of Dutch kitchens. Most were carpenter-built, often of a height that insured their destruction when they could not fit out the door. Usually of pine, they were painted in various colors, usually orange within and a blue or red outside, this one in Prussian blue. The common orange pigment was red lead; the Dutch did not realize it was hazardous.

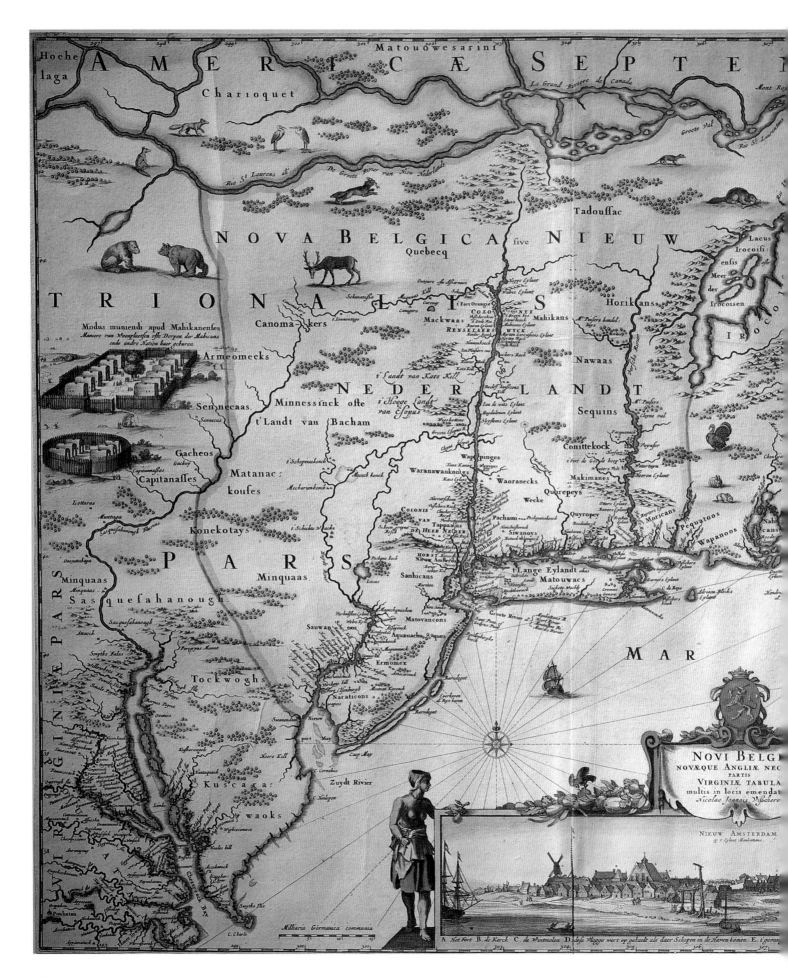

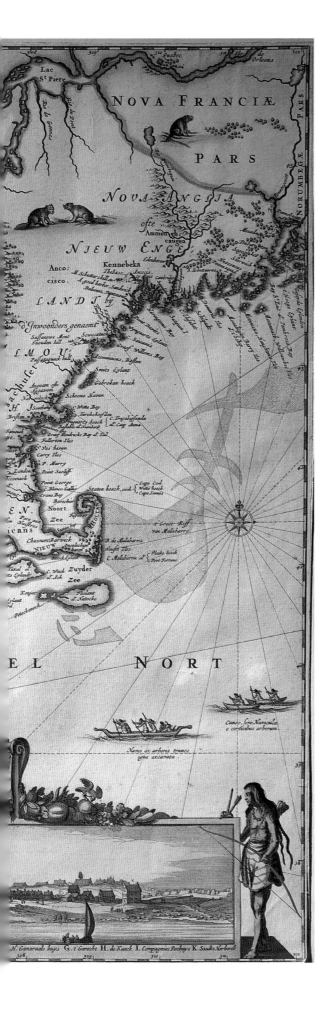

New Netherland

The Claes Janszoon Visscher Map, first state, 1650/51

1650, Private collection

This is the first state of a map of New Netherland issued in 1650 or 1651 by Amsterdam cartographer Claes Janszoon Visscher. The inset view of New Amsterdam (New York City) was copied from an etched view issued by Johannes Bleau in 1650 based on a sketch of New Amsterdam done there in 1648 as an accompaniment to Adriaen van der Donk's Remonstrance of New Netherland. It was presented to the States-General in the Hague in 1649. The original 1648 sketch was discovered in 1991. The place names of even minor settlements are carefully inscribed, many still in use today. The density of their presence along rivers and bays eloquently states the nature of mobility in the seventeenth century—mostly by water. It was a rare Dutchman who wandered far from water to settle, a legacy of his water-born homeland and the practicality of moving anything by boat rather than over hilly, seasonally rutted roads. The pattern of Dutch settlement in early America is topographically predictable: most are villages near the confluence of interior streams and navigable rivers; farms are near streams along alluvial flatlands; and houses are on the first rise above those streams.

The Claes Janszoon Visscher map—detail of New York harbor.

A History
of the Colonial Dutch

New Netherland

The Netherlands was a small nation that became rich and powerful beyond its size because of trade. In the late 1500s the Dutch, newly freed and independent from Spanish tyranny, fostered ambitions to extend The Netherlands' influence and commerce—primarily by trade rather than force of arms—throughout the world. The story began with Hendrick Hudson's unsuccessful search for a trade route to the orient in the employ of the Dutch East India Company and his exploration of the river subsequently named for him. Early reports extolling the attractiveness of the land and climate along with the willingness of the native inhabitants to barter desirable furs for manufactured goods immediately inspired Dutch traders to send ships to this region. However, competitive disputes ensued. In 1621, the governing body of The Netherlands—called the States General—wanted to establish order in the region and granted exclusive authority to the Dutch West India Company. The company, privately owned by shareholders, governed the colony of New Netherland. It assumed responsibility for judicial, legislative, and administrative control of much of what later became Connecticut, Delaware, New Jersey, and New York. This timely follow-up on Hudson's discoveries enabled the Dutch to establish trading outposts in the region, which they called New Netherland, before their commercial competitors from England and France.

The Dutch West India Company made half-hearted attempts to encourage settlement beginning in about 1624. Thirty families were initially brought over to establish an agricultural base to support the company's fur trade. Inducing enough families to come to this wilderness was a daunting task. While a bountiful land by all accounts, it was still a feared place. Life at the remote outpost required a brave heart and demanded hard work. Because all of the manufactured necessities of life had to be imported, colonization proved to be very expensive for the company. Furthermore it was difficult to recruit Dutch settlers even among the poorest classes at a time when conditions in The Netherlands were among the most prosperous in Europe. When people from other nations less economically success-ful or less socially tolerant than The Netherlands showed an interest in immigration they were accepted. The result was that the small colonial population was as much foreign as Dutch.

The early colonists were mostly young single men who worked for the Dutch West India Company or were farmers, craftsmen, laborers, and servants. A number of the settlers were also shopkeepers and independent traders. Many who came hoped the fur trade would make them rich. The majority were seeking a place in the new land to bring a wife and start a family. It is their story over the subsequent two centuries that identifies them as a distinct people.

Almost immediately the promise of lucrative trade with the natives resulted in complications. The first group of settlers had been sent in small groups to the far reaches of the colony. Within two years the Dutch West India Company recalled them to Manhattan for their safety. It was the beginning of a fitful accommodation with local tribes punctuated with misunderstandings, disagreements, culturally different perceptions of land ownership and use, and the eventual over-exploitation of fur animals. The ineptitude and avarice of the Company's directors precipitated a significant part of the colony's problems. Word of a series of armed conflicts between the two groups reached the homeland, discouraging immigration. Ironically the impact caused by war and disease upon the Native Americans was even more devastating, causing a long decline in their population. This was the beginning of trends that resulted in more land becoming available for colonization—a pattern that characterized settlement on the American frontier for centuries.

Not wishing to expend shareholder money to recruit immigrants, the company, with the concurrence of the States General in The Netherlands, passed the costs for settlement to individual patroons. The 1629 Charter of Freedoms and Exemptions was designed to encourage settlement by granting what were called patroonships to companies or individuals. Patroons were given land if they agreed to settle fifty people within a set period of time. The promise of thousands of acres for merely settling a few rent-paying tenants induced several to apply and receive such a grant. A successful patroonship was Rensselaerswyck. But even with a million acres surrounding the frontier outpost called Fort Orange, later Albany, it took the Van Rensselaer family—charter members of the company and wealthy diamond merchants in their own right—over a century to realize substantial profits.

As part of a series of worldwide struggles for commercial and colonial supremacy the Dutch were relentlessly pressured on all fronts. The company's more vital interests in other parts of the world including the Caribbean, Brazil, and Africa caused it to neglect New Netherland, as it showed less immediate promise of profits. Commercial competition

between England and The Netherlands resulted in the First Anglo-Dutch War in the 1650s. New Netherland was saved by the terms of the Treaty of Westminster that ended the war in 1654. That benevolent intercession merely delayed the inevitable. The dilemma of New Netherland—a paucity of people in a land of natural plenty—proved its undoing. The company lost effective control of the eastern border of the colony along the Connecticut River Valley in the 1650s as English settlers began to outnumber the Dutch. Later in the 1650s, company director-general Petrus Stuyvesant only temporarily stemmed the loss of the Delaware Valley to Sweden by military action.

In 1663, the newly restored King of England, Charles II, decided to eliminate the Dutch presence in North

The Claes Janszoon Visscher map—detail of Fort Orange region.

The Claes Janszoon Visscher map—detail of view of fort and church.

America. In 1664 neighboring New England's population was over six times that of New Netherland. When English settlements were established within eighteen miles of New Amsterdam (now New York City), the tiny Dutch colony began to be overwhelmed. Outnumbered by New Englanders and outgunned by the British navy whose fleet entered New Amsterdam harbor in September 1664, the municipality was boldly taken without a fight, as was what was left of the colony. In one stroke King Charles quieted the New England clamor for this fertile, under-populated Dutch colony and gave the newly acquired province to his brother, the future King James II.

The Dutch Legacy

The apparent failure of a Dutch colony has ever since masked a series of accomplishments that subtly survived a century of English control to influence the most important principles on which our nation was founded. While we see around us the material survivals of this lost culture—Dutch houses and barns and their furnishings—we should now view them as emblematic reminders of important gifts to our own society. Among these are: The early establishment of law courts and chartered town governments; the beginning of public representation in government; and public responsibility for the relief of the poor.

Dutch laws also effected America's future principals. The Pacification of Ghent in 1576 and the Peace of Religion in 1577 acknowledged freedom of religious worship. The Union of Utrecht—the founding law of the United Provinces of The Netherlands of 1579—was an inspiration for the first proposal of union among the colonies, set forth at an inter-colonial conference at Albany in 1754 by Benjamin Franklin. This was the precursor of the Articles of Confederation and that, in turn, of the Constitution of the United States under which we live today. It is interesting to note that The Dutch Act of Abjuration of 1581 that declared Dutch freedom from Spanish subjugation has wording remarkably similar to Thomas Jefferson's draft of the Declaration of Independence.

In each of these precedents we see foundation stones of governing principles subsequently set forth in America's Declaration of Independence and Constitution, including the Bill of Rights. Here are models for our federal structure, for rights of faith and conscience, and for freedom from tyranny. Unfortunately much of this remarkable legacy of our Dutch heritage goes unrecognized today.

An English Dukedom

The charter King Charles gave his brother James, Duke of York and Albany, was remarkable for the powers granted. The duke did not have to contend with a representative assembly as was established in the New England colonies. He could make and regulate all appointments, laws, trade, defense, and land grants. In fact he was potentially quite absolute in his powers. In practice, though, James' rule was relatively benign. All residents, excepting slaves, continued as "free denizens" regardless of nationality. Property rights were secure, even those of the Dutch West India Company, although a direct relationship with The Netherlands was forbidden. The Dutch were allowed their traditional patterns of inheritance, contracts, and choices of magistrates. Although he was a Catholic governing a mostly Protestant colony, the Duke guaranteed freedom of conscience and freedom of worship. It was a far more liberal policy than Governor Stuyvesant had tolerated.

In matters of land tenure, the Duke's governors ratified the existing Dutch land grants. They also created a quiltwork of many new manors throughout the Hudson Valley. In addition to land, the tenure system gave privileges over

Engraved portrait of a Mohawk (Iroquois) Indian, 1710.

other wealth-building opportunities in the form of monopolies and concessions that engendered the development of a small upper class of manorial landlords. Although the grantees who owned most of the lands in the colony were of Dutch decent, all remained beholden to the English government for access to political power. However, these men soon consolidated their power by becoming closely allied by marriage and business to the wealthy merchant families of New York and Albany. Cemented by kinship ties, this tightly knit affluent group operated more like a well-regulated Anglo-Dutch clan than a money-defined class. The manorial system had the far-reaching effect of slowing immigration and economic growth. Settlement in the Hudson Valley languished through the eighteenth century as settlers were attracted to colonies offering more favorable terms of land tenure: most prospective settlers preferred to acquire land not subject to lease terms and title renewals. These settlers wanted the security of clear freehold titles and the ability to pass land and farm improvements onto their heirs.

> As the Dutch, who first cultivated this section, obtained the liberty of staying here by the treaty with England, and of enjoying all their privileges and advantages without the least limitation, … Most of them being very rich, their envy of the English led them not to sell any land, but at an excessive rate, a practice which is still punctually observed among their descendants. The English therefore, as well as people of other nations, have but little encouragement to settle here.
> —Peter Kalm, 1748 [*Travels*, p. 143]

Imperial Rivalries

In Europe, the French and English had been enemies off and on for centuries, seeking advantage in diplomacy or, if necessary, war to insure their claims to land and commerce throughout the world, but especially in North America where both coveted control. The French in Canada and the Dutch (and later the English) in New York, vied for hegemony over the wealth of the wilderness and the Native Americans who supplied them with furs. These were the primary geo-political issues of colonial America.

For two hundred years the powerful Iroquois Confederacy controlled the balance of power between the colonial powers. Whoever held their allegiance could control both the fur trade and the Hudson-Champlain Valley's invasion route south from Canada to New York City. Theoretically, control of this corridor was seen as a wedge that could split New England from the rest of the English colonies and lead to the conquest of all North America. That was the strategy of the French and British and throughout the four Anglo-French wars, the Revolution, and the War of 1812 (and an aborted war in the 1830s), New York was frequently at the center of the action.

Nevertheless, the New York Dutch were reluctant participants in these imperial rivalries. The peace and prosperity they had once fostered was repeatedly jeopardized by the fear or fact of war from the late seventeenth to the early nineteenth centuries. They were caught up in this rivalry and it affected their relations with all other groups both within and outside of the colony. New York, the primary scene of colonial frontier battles over many generations, became the anvil upon which colonial men including the Dutch, who hardly ventured beyond their farms or local towns, were forged into Americans. Wars or community controversies formed new and deeper relationships resulting in an increased sense of community identity among allied individuals and families. Community identity, of course, is also built upon more considered foundations, both concrete and spiritual.

Faith, Family, and Fortune

The rock of Dutch identity throughout the colonial period and beyond was, and still is, the Reformed Church. It is the last surviving institution of this culture, and it has been, excepting the family itself, the most important. It was the outward and visible arena in which and by which the Dutch consciously maintained their Dutchness in the face of all other ethnic, religious, and political encroachments—first from the Anglican English and then from the Roman Catholic French.

As the leading institution in a community, the Reformed Church came to serve other subtle purposes. With the

Engraved view of the Dutch Church in New York, by William Burgis, 1731

blessing of a higher authority (God) and the coaching of determined dominies (ministers), the Church helped sustain Dutch separate identity by perpetuating their language, faith, and life-cycle rituals. While meeting at church for worship, civic leaders of Dutch descent often considered broader community issues under cover of their own building and within the secrecy of their own language. Despite a century of accommodation to, and even benefit from, English rule, it was Dominie Westerlo in Albany who harangued his congregation about the frivolous distractions of English customs and into defiance of the British during the Revolution.

The Reformed Church, like other voluntary institutions, was also vulnerable. The congregations' mundane concerns begat controversies as they argued over issues of interpretation and authority, as well as issues of funding their church and selecting and working with their dominies. Congregations in New York and New Jersey through much of the eighteenth century argued and sometimes split over issues such as whether dominies could be ordained in the colony, allowed to preach in English, or be pietistic or orthodox. It affected who people worshipped with, who they married, and where they lived. In some ways these factors also affected how they lived and the homes they built.

Like faith and community, the nuclear family was indispensable to the Dutch. Among the Dutch, and to varying degrees with other colonial groups, the family was the primary institution for civilizing purposes. Dutch children not only received their socializing in the family, they often received most of their education therein, as well as their introduction into productive life. Boys were often contracted out as apprentices to learn and live with a tradesman, still in the bosom of a family. After seven years each apprentice became a journeyman and was permitted to practice his trade on his own. A young man could then marry and establish his own household. Boys of wealthier families may have had an opportunity for further schooling yet many also became apprentices, often in a mercantile business.

Even among wealthy Dutch families, the concept of training in a manual skill—a skill by which one could earn an income no matter the future—was deeply ingrained. Young Killiaen Van Rensselaer (1663–1719), for example, although the scion of this most landed of all New York families, was apprenticed to an unidentified silversmith in New York from 1678–82. Qualified as a journeyman, he sought further training in Boston under silversmith Jeremiah Dummer. Colonial silversmiths, while trained to a manual craft, were often prominent community members compared to other craftsmen. Young Van Rensselaer's promising career was cut short when he prematurely inherited the Manor of Rensselaerswyck.

Daughters were more often raised in their natal families, learning household skills. There are records of some being apprenticed while others, probably from more prosperous families, spent part of their youth in related families, all primarily for the same purpose—to become proper mistresses for their own households upon marriage. Who they married was not only of concern to themselves and their prospective partners, but also to their parents.

In this colonial society advancement in life may have come from personal skill and determination, but it more assuredly could come from family wealth and connections since relatively few positions were available in which to attain rank and/or wealth in government, the army, corporations, or social institutions. What a young Dutch gentleman could look forward to if he was from a well-off family, albeit a distinct minority, was a position in the family business, usually trade. The family took on heightened importance in Dutch society especially among the more patrician families. It was a prime vehicle for creating and sustaining wealth. Wealth begat advantageous family connections and thereby preference in business, politics, and the army or militia.

In those days gaining wealth from one's official position (in addition to a salary) was expected and condoned. As a colonial officer approving land grants, for example, one could expect to be included in a share—often a silent share—of the grant. Wealth was also obtained in the army, particularly for those who received (either by merit, connection, or payment) a quartermaster position. Quartermasters bought supplies for the troops and pocketed commissions as they went. This was a widespread and accepted traditional perk of office of that time. The colonial Dutch and English were both much practiced in these affairs from the old country. Those of Dutch descent who saw advantage in allying themselves with British administrators benefited handsomely in this way and built the finest houses, usually in the English fashion.

The institution of land grants was the principal vehicle of speculation in colonial New York. Leading families became

Detail from Burgis view of Albany, c.1718–21,
showing boat, stockade, church, and urban Dutch houses.

rich, at least land rich, although often cash poor. It took the Van Renssealaer's, owners of Rensselaerswyck, a century before they could move out of a virtual farmhouse and into a mansion. For those rich in land, an advantageous marriage to a cash-rich trading family was desirable. Urban families may have owned land and a fine house, but they had originally made their wealth by foresight and entrepreneurial spirit. They had seen advantages in buying commodities like furs and produce at home, and then selling them in the Caribbean or Europe to purchase slaves and sugar in the West Indies or finished goods in England which they could then sell at home. This network of trade, on which the Dutch had founded their society centuries before and by which they became the wealthiest people in Europe, dovetailed neatly with their system of family alliances. This conjunction applied especially to the wealthy Anglo-Dutch, but we can see it replicated in the middle and lower ranks of society among the city and town merchants, the tradesmen, and the outlying farm families.

Since a sizable percent of the population made its living off the land it is no surprise that almost all the buildings illustrated in this book were on farms (and some still are). If one did a genealogical investigation of the link-ages among the families who lived in these houses (as Helen Wilkinson Reynolds and especially Rosalie Fellows Bailey did in their seminal books on the Dutch and their houses, see Bibliography), one would see how inter-connected they were by marriage as much as by physical proximity and faith.

Evolution
of the Dutch House

The Medieval Experience

We can explain many features of Dutch colonial life if we examine the institutions of governance, faith, family, and commerce by which people were organized to pursue their lives. While the Dutch nation is relatively modern, Dutch culture dates back to the Middle Ages where we can find the beginnings of this way of life. Explaining how and why the Dutch built their houses as they did also involves going back to the origins of their medieval way of life to unfold the layers of their historic experience.

The evolution of the house in Western Europe is a story of structures as well as how people lived in them and what they sought from them. That has changed over the centuries yet retained much of its ancient form right up to the modern era. The Middle Ages began a millennium ago yet attributes of that life lasted in some places into the twentieth century. The type of houses which originated then were built almost as long and survive in numbers today, both in Europe and America.

Early on, houses were but a single hall, the furnishing being sparse out of economy of money and of space for everyone to live in. Everything happened in this room and everyone used it. It was more public than private, a place you camped in more than lived in. The center of life was the hearth, a fire in the middle of a dirt floor. Through the day and night furniture was moved about to accommodate a succession of functions: food preparation, eating, meeting of guests, doing business, sleeping, etc. ". . . of comfort there was little, and, being unknown, it was unmissed." commented Walter Scott.

As they lived differently, they also thought differently. Medieval life had a different culture. While today we think of furnishings by how they look or are used, back then they saw most everything for its associated meanings within their divinely ordered world. We might call it superstition, but in their mind everything and everyone had emblematic significance and unseen functions beyond the mere utilitarian. If I do differently, thinks the medieval merchant, what will God think? What will the priest say? The local lord do? The

neighbors whisper about? The hag witch do to me? My wife reprove me? To us these are invisible and irrelevant constraints, but to them (and in tribal societies today) such constraints on behavior and innovation are real. There were positive sides to these fears, there was comfort in conformity because it was safe. Such strong beliefs in the power of the supernatural, whether divinely or humanly exercised, held tenaciously for centuries once established in a culture. We can sense it still persisting among the early colonists in the New World who still believed in witches and ghosts (we have not quite separated ourselves from the latter). They continued to build and live in essentially medieval houses well into the eighteenth century precisely because this was comforting to their beliefs. The colonial Dutch knew of a more modern life style and elegant homes being advanced by the leading English and Anglo/Dutch citizens of their colony beginning in the late seventeenth century, but that did not ease their conscience into accepting these new ways. Change meant much more than changing houses and dress, it meant giving up a way of life long sanctioned by their God-fearing belief in their ancestral ways.

This does not mean that Dutch ways were frozen in a medieval time warp. Dutch houses did change by adaptation to New World conditions: new materials, new occupations, and new political realities. The pioneer hovel evolved from one- and two-, to three- and four-room houses. The fireplace moved to the wall, its smoke captured by a chimney. Rooms began to have separate functions. For example, one room continued as an all-purpose, semi-public room, and another evolved into one for special occasions and for the master and wife who, for privacy, began to withdraw from the children and servants.

This was the beginning of a march towards domesticity in the home which occurred over much of Europe and in the colonies, first in the upper classes in the seventeenth century and then later, sometimes much later, among the rural peasantry. Furniture began to become decorative and valuable, not just utilitarian. Some rooms became show rooms and privacy increased by adding new rooms.

In European palaces this was an ongoing process, as each private room took on more public and showy purposes while more intimate rooms were added. In the colonies the progression can be seen by the addition of attached or separate kitchens followed by the innovation of the central hall which made true privacy possible: For the first time a room could be closed off from others and was not needed to get to other rooms. In New York and New Jersey, this was the beginning of the newer style house. While it was a product of English ideas, its adoption depended on a higher level of affluence to both build such expensive structures and to maintain them. Separate bedrooms each needed fireplaces making it necessary for servants to cut, store, and bring in wood and then tend the fires and remove ashes. This was required constantly in winter.

As the Dutch began to prosper in eighteenth-century New York they could afford such houses and their cultural beliefs began to shift such that they could accept giving up their old ways. This was a slow progression emanating out from New York City which took a century to happen in remote places like the upper Hudson River valley, while regions closer to the city, such as nearby Bergen and Monmouth Counties in New Jersey and Kings and Queens Counties on Long Island, experienced more rapid acculturation.

The Dutch House Today

Dutch houses are a curiosity to look upon and a delight to discover. They are isolated from each other, tucked away on abandoned farms or hidden in suburban developments among newer houses. They are the only reminders of our colonial past which we may casually and unexpectedly come upon; all other Dutch artifacts are tucked away in museums, libraries, and private collections. As such, they have a public presence that inspires curiosity about how these houses came to be, how they worked, and why they were built as they were. It is possible to "read" a house like a book, to interpret its features like an archeologist.

Reading a house involves layers of understanding. At first one sees its form, the arrangement of spaces and coverings such as the walls, ceilings, and roof. Next noticed is its style, how the form is expressed in features and finishes such as the size, shape, details, and arrangements of windows, doors, walls, roof and decorative features. Understanding the house often stops here with an explanation of the national or ethnic origin of the form and style. But the observer can go further by looking into the functions of the Dutch house, how it worked and how the needs of its owners and of the structure itself caused changes in the Dutch house over time. Form, style, and function are interrelated; almost any change in one affecting the others.

In colonial New York and New Jersey many houses were first built as single-room structures. Soon some were built as one-room-and-a-hall houses or with two identical rooms. Later houses had two rooms with a hall between them, and still later ones were built with a central hall and two rooms on either side. The advent of these large houses saw the beginning of upstairs bedrooms. Alterations to these existing houses also began early in the colonial period. Pioneer one-room houses expanded into two, three, four and more rooms that were arranged in a number of ways. Many Dutch houses show the development of their use by how and why additions were made to the original house. For example, a one-room house could also have a new two-room house added to it, the old house becoming a secondary—often called "summer" or "out"-kitchen. In other cases the one-room house remained as a separate kitchen. The desire for such a secondary kitchen was so widespread that if the first house was, say, a two-room house, one room being a kitchen, an attached or separate kitchen was still added (p. 91). In the summer, this extra kitchen made it possible to avoid unwelcome heat and smells in the main house, conditions that were tolerated and, sometimes, desirable in the winter.

As houses became deeper and higher their form and style changed, reflecting structural necessities caused by this enlargement. For example, the shape and underlying structure of the roof changed to accommodate room enlargement. Early Dutch houses were usually one-room deep covered by a high-pitch roof with steep slanting sides (pp. 56-7). That was fine for narrow houses but a steep-pitch roof over a large house created such a high roof that it became vulnerable to wind stresses (p.127). The solution was to either build the roof structure stronger with extra bracing (*right*) or adapt a lower type of roof—the gambrel roof with two slants to a side, the upper slant being quite low (p. 99). This lowered the roof yet preserved the same usable headroom in the upper floor. The gambrel roof was not a Netherlands feature, but was borrowed from the English in New England and, quite possibly, from the influence of Huguenots—French Protestants who settled in New York and New Jersey.

Besides size, room arrangement, and roof form, the material of construction is another obvious exterior feature of Dutch houses. Their homes were built with walls either covered with wood weatherboards or brick, or made of stone—and often a combination of two. The choice of materials depended on a Dutchman's means, taste, and the availability of materials and skilled workmen.

Not as visible was the cellar, the last section of a house. Unlike walls and a roof, it was not a necessity and some houses did not have them. A cellar was desirable as a place of storage, though, and if it had a kitchen, was a place for work and sometimes habitation.

. . . this is how the houses belonging to the Dutch living in the country were built. They first put up the framework upon which the rafters and both roofs rested and then filled in the framework with unfired bricks. The inner side was brushed over with lime and whitewashed so that from the inside it looked like a stone house except where the perpendicular timbers which supported the rafters were visible. On the outside the houses were generally covered with clapboards so that the unfired brick might not be damaged by moisture, weather and wind. As a rule they did not have more perpendicular supports in the walls than they had cross beams, from three to five on each side or long wall . . . . The ceiling was horizontal and beamed. The roof was either of boards or shingles; there were several rooms under one roof. —Peter Kalm, 1749–50 [*Travels*, p. 611]

A cellar with a kitchen was outfitted just like the one on the floor above with a similar if smaller open fireplace, its flue

Beams and braces, Jean Hasbrouck House, New Paltz, NY.

stepped out on the gable wall to bypass the fireplace above (p. 131). Being a room of habitation even though in the cellar, its woodwork, namely the ceiling beams and floorboards, were as smoothly finished (and just as devoid of paint) as those in the rooms above (p. 82). At the back of this room and through a door there was usually a store room, its ceiling beams rough-finished. How exposed woodwork such as ceiling beams and floorboards were finished—either smooth or rough—is an indicator of whether the room was intended for habitation or just for storage. As will be discussed later (p. 42), the placement of windows adjacent to fireplaces was also an indicator of how interior spaces were used.

European Antecedents of Colonial Houses

Dutch Colonial houses were closely related in certain features to those found in The Netherlands that date back to medieval times. In both, houses consisted of one or two

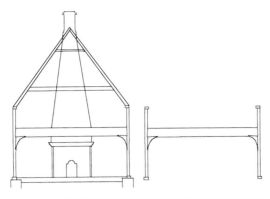

D1 H-Bent Frame,
Van Alen House,
Kinderhook, NY.

Garret Interior Gable,
The Leendert Bronck
House, Coxsackie, NY.

Dutch Fireplace,
Roeloff Westervelt
House, Tenafly, NJ.

D2 Dutch Fireplace,
Van Alen House,
Kinderhook, NY.

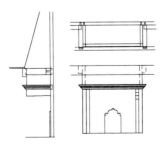

rooms enclosed by a structure of wall posts supporting a set of parallel ceiling beams. Each set of two wall posts and interconnected deep beams formed the **H** frame or "bent" (*see diagram* D1). Four or five of these bents enclosed a room and all the bents were held together by a beam called a plate that went across the top of each set of wall posts. All the posts in a wall rested upon a sill beam at floor level. Rafters forming the roof began on the two long plates and met at the ridge. Pairs of rafters were, like the bents below, joined together at the top or apex of the roof with an open mortise and tenon joint and also by another beam called a collar tie. These three members formed a rigid triangular framework (*left*) countering wind pressure and the outward splaying pressure of a snow or ice load. Rafters were covered by roofing boards called sheathing on which shingles were nailed (some houses were once covered with thatch or pantiles). Walls were covered with wood boards called weatherboards (distinct from smaller clapboards used in New England). Some houses were enclosed with brick veneer; brick walls were not load-bearing since the wall posts held up the structure. Other houses had stone walls. Because of the irregularity of rubble stone these walls could not be fitted neatly around wall posts so they were built thick, holding up the structure without the use of wall posts, a colonial innovation made by the Dutch. Lastly, most houses were supported on stone foundation walls enclosing a cellar, partially below ground.

In each full-size room, Dutch houses had a unique type of fireplace (p. 64, *left*) set against a wall with little or no sides (or jambs). The smoke would rise into a hood-shaped chimney (p. 123) of bricks resting on a framework composed of the deep fireplace beam and two trimmer beams joining it to the wall beam (D2). This type of fireplace was a feature that went back centuries in northern Europe, evolving from the medieval peasant house in which a hearth was set in the middle of a dirt floor without a chimney above, the smoke merely seeping through the thatch roof. In time the hearth was reset to a side wall and still later a chimney—like a hanging hood—was built above it. The medieval-house framework and fireplace continued to be built until the middle of the eighteenth century in some areas of New York.

These basic features of Dutch houses distinguish them from other colonial houses derived from other national origins. New England houses derived their form from yeoman houses built in England, also from medieval times. The English house is characterized by a central chimney with multiple flues for fireplaces in each room on two floors and in the cellar. The structural system is composed in each room of a large beam in the ceiling called a girt or summer beam from which smaller joists radiated out to the walls. In all it was a complex frame requiring a bewildering variety of joints, resulting in rooms of different shape and structure. This is a much more complex house to build than the simple H frame Dutch house.

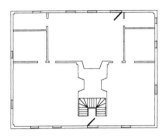

D3 New England House

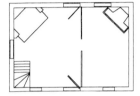

D4 Swedish House

The New England house evolved, like others, from a small rectangular one-room house with a large fireplace in a gable wall. This was offset to the side to give space for a small vestibule for the entry door. These were one-story houses (a story-and-a-half in Rhode Island). The next phase was to increase the height to two stories, then to double the house by adding a room to the other side of the fireplace wall thus creating a central entry to a stairway vestibule and a central chimney with two fireplaces on each floor (D3). With the increase in height, an overhanging second floor became common, a trait which may have once had a function in England to protect the surface of half-timbered walls but in New England, where walls were covered with weather-tight clapboards, was just a vestigial decoration.

The next step was to add a lean-to to the rear of the house creating a large kitchen and fireplace, and two unheated rooms—a bedroom and pantry—on either end. This type of house looked like the New England "salt box," giving a name to this lean-to form. By adding the lean-to, lost space was created in the rear attic. In time, the upstairs was turned into the same room arrangement as below and the roof raised in the rear to accommodate this, thus moving the ridge backward to the center of the house.

By the late seventeenth century, a last major change was made among the most fashionable: the house was expanded by a center stair hall. This allowed for a large, well-lighted—instead of tightly wound—stairway and enabled full circulation to all four rooms, not just those in the front. The central chimney became two separate ones on interior longitudinal partition walls. Back-to-back fireplaces accessed all rooms. There were concomitant changes in all the other features to go with the room changes: steep-pitch roofs became shallower or gambrel; casements became sash windows; the front door took on elaborate architectonic pilasters and pediments; the interior was festooned with paneled cupboards and walls; and the ceiling was covered with plaster. This process of evolution of the New England house was to play an important part in later changes in Dutch houses.

In the Delaware Valley of western New Jersey and eastern Pennsylvania a seventeenth-century Swedish colony was established. The Swedes brought the log home with corner fireplaces to America. Their houses had one or two rooms; the latter was a large square room and a small adjacent room with an outside door (D4). While their houses are nearly all gone, their log-house concept was adopted by the Dutch and English who came to this region in the late seventeenth century. William Penn specifically recommended to settlers a

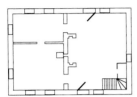

D5 German House

house plan that was essentially Swedish. In the hands of Quakers, the original plan was expanded to include three and four rooms and hallways, yet for a long time the houses retained Swedish attributes.

Germans also came to Penn's colony, bringing with them a house type closely related to their place of origin, the Palatinate region of the Rhine Valley (Alsace, Reinpfalz and Baden). Their influence is especially obvious in exterior features, particularly the cove cornice that extended the roof line outward from the wall and, below that, at the first-floor level of these one-and-a-half or two-story houses, a pent roof extending two or three feet from the wall. Both originated in the Rhine Valley to protect non-masonry walls, that is, log and half-timbered buildings common to that region. While not necessary for weatherboard or stone-wall houses, they were useful in protecting the caulked walls of hewn log houses.

They built their houses in eastern Pennsylvania and down the Great Valley into Virginia and as far as western South Carolina. The idea of the cove eave and pent roof persisted through the eighteenth century, widely adopted by Quakers on both sides of the Delaware River. The basic plan of the German house included two deep rooms, one with a large kitchen fireplace on the inner partition wall, a stairway winding in the outer corner of the room, and a front door adjacent to it (D5). Two large beams laid from gable end to fireplace wall, each holding many smaller joists, held the ceiling. Doors on either side of the fireplace provided access to the smaller room, which was divided into a square front room and a smaller room behind it; a partition was placed

between them. The larger of these smaller rooms had a five-plate stove connecting to the fireplace in the main room.

There are some common threads to the evolution of these European-derived houses. All are based on northern European medieval building traditions and all were reinterpreted in colonial America on a frontier that initially had modest means but an abundance of resources. In addition, all evolved from one- and two-room houses into a New Style house with center hall and multiple rooms on two floors. The New Style was based on a post-medieval way of living which spread through Europe and then America, changing the way people of means saw their lives and the way they wished to live—ideals which are still with us today.

These widespread changes coincided with changes in the accepted view of the individual's place in the world, embracing the Enlightenment's view of the free will of individuals and of democracy. The idea of the primacy of the individual advanced notions of personal privacy which were translated into separate bedrooms for each. The acceptance of these ideas in America was advanced by the Enlightenment views of our founding fathers—views which, as we have seen, derive in part from principles of social justice espoused by the people of The Netherlands.

Dutch Houses: Urban and Rural

Rural houses make up the majority of homes photographed in this book. That's because more of these farm houses still exist today. There were Dutch houses in towns and cities but they are now almost all gone or have been altered. These urban homes had somewhat different arrangements than those described previously. This was caused by the necessity of building houses close together within tightly confined, fortified walls. Narrow end and entrance doors faced the street and the side walls butted against the houses on either side; in some cases houses shared the same wall. Rural houses, on the other hand, could make ample use of long side walls to bring in light and air through multiple windows and doors. For this reason, they are oriented to the side, making

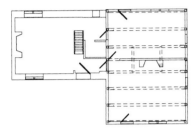

D6 Pieter Winnie House,
Bethlehem, NY.

them look quite different even though they share the same characteristics of structure and style as urban houses. To illustrate the contrast we can look at two rural houses built in the urban-house form (D6) (p. 74, p. 86) with gable end entrances, quite different from the conventional side-entrance farmhouse (p. 214).

In New Amsterdam (New York City) some early urban houses and warehouses were built unusually large and do not survive except in pictures. Their size was expressed in height, the one direction of expansion possible in a tightly organized stockaded town. Some were several floors in elevation, although rarely more than twenty-feet wide.

In the countryside of New Netherland there was another type of structure, the rural barn/house. The farmer's family lived in one end of a barn structure and domestic stock, hay, and grain were stored in the other portion. Judging from building contracts dating from the seventeenth century these were large structures: one from 1641 was as large as ninety by twenty-four feet. Like large urban structures, these have long since disappeared from our country but can still be seen in The Netherlands.

The Functions of Dutch Houses

To understand function, it's important to outline some basic requirements of houses: first, houses must be strong and tight enough to withstand the elements; next, houses must be economical, affordable, and efficient to build, repair, and maintain; third, houses must protect residents and their possessions, and keep dwellers healthy; last, houses must be

comfortable, that is, residents and their possessions need to be accommodated in a convenient number of rooms of proper size in which the temperature is regulated. Houses function properly if they are economical, comfortable, and afford protection for human work and habitation.

Across the world societies have produced many types of houses to meet people's ideas of what constitutes economy, comfort, and protection. These variations in any one society, like the New World Dutch, result from local differences in natural resources, topography, climate, and ethnic settlement. Examining the specific ways the Dutch sought to answer these three prerequisites can provide enlightenment about why they built their houses as they did.

A discussion of how a house survives is another important topic. A house survives when it is built in a dry and well-drained location. Its roof must shed rain and snow away from walls and foundations to keep the house dry and slow the growth of rot; this is why houses have gutters or overhanging eaves. The roof material (tile, wood shingles, or thatch) must be tight enough to shed moisture quickly, so that leaks and rot do not occur.

A house's structural system (the interlocking posts and beams, rafters, and braces) must be strong enough to withstand external elements (snow and ice loading) and internal weighting (furniture, people, and storage). This weighting requires adequately strong floor beams and floorboards. A house also needs to be rigid enough to withstand wind pressure. A house needs strong wall posts (or stone walls) joined to ceiling beams which are sometimes braced with corbels for added rigidity. These are topped by plates (horizontal beams) which hold up the rafters of the roof. Rafters are also made rigid by collar beams and diagonal braces, securing the whole against wind from any direction. The taller the roof the more bracing it requires.

Roofing materials and the related pitch or steepness of the roof had a significant effect on the type of house the Dutch built. A roof must shed rain and snow and protect the house from the damages of ice buildup. For this, a roof requires a secure and weatherproof roofing material. In The Netherlands, largely devoid of wood for shingles, the Dutch used (and still use) fired clay pantiles and thatch. Pantiles work best when laid on a steep roof so that wind is less likely to drive rain or snow under the loosely laid pantiles. On the other hand, if laid too steeply wind can blow pantiles off the roof, since they are secured only by gravity. Long ago, the Dutch came up with the ideal roof angle—fifty-six degrees. They also made thatch from reeds, a roofing material which lasts longer when laid steeply enough so rain runs off quickly and does not soak in (which rots the reeds). Both materials made it necessary for Dutch roofs to be built at a steep angle.

When the Dutch came to America they continued to build steep roofs using their traditional materials. In a new land covered with plentiful trees, the Dutch began to use tight, nailed-down wood shingles which did not require a steep roof. Gradually the Dutch began to lower the roof angle of their houses, but not as quickly as shingles allowed. Old ways died slowly, a millennium of building steep roofs made them visually "right" even if functionally no longer essential. One useful indicator of the age of a Dutch house is the pitch of the roof; the lower it is, the later it was built. Shingle roofs became popular on farmhouses by the mid-seventeenth century.

In addition to the functional requirements of a roof and walls, a house needs a foundation to support it and to prevent ground moisture from seeping in. Some rudimentary houses rested on a few sill stones; others were built on wood post foundations enclosed by boards against the ground, guaranteed to rot out in a generation. Most houses, however, were built with full cellars. These had to have stone walls thick enough to resist the pressure of expanding frozen ground, tight enough to repel ground moisture, and strong enough to support the structure above, especially if stone. For these reasons, almost all houses were built with rubble stone—stone of mixed natural size—either dry laid, but more often mortared tight. If ground water was high, the cellar was built partially above ground. If built into a hill,

one side could have a ground-level entrance, especially convenient for a cellar kitchen. High foundations also allowed ample windows for ventilation and light. These openings into the house—the doors and windows—had another function; they were designed to be tight and waterproof to help regulate temperature and control moisture.

Lastly, a house must be built of what is available and, equally important, affordable. Here we see a trade-off between affordability and desirability. Wood siding was cheaper but was less weather-proof or long lasting, more prone to fire damage, and more high-maintenance. Brick and stone were weather tight and more fireproof, but brick, while elegant, was more expensive. Local resources limited choices: wood was available in all areas; stone and brick only in some areas.

Like structures themselves, residents also had requirements or needs. Certainly security was paramount. The adage "a man's home is his castle" sums it up well, expressing a desire and pride in ownership as well as a concern for safety from enemies and elements. It also implies the importance of privacy. Residents' next concern was for comfort—having a well-lit space with suitable furnishings, as well as enough rooms, properly arranged, with adequate space. Residents also sought convenience—the efficient arrangement of space and structural features to complete activities such as cooking, eating, sleeping, and entertaining, and to meet privacy needs and storage requirements. They also desired to live in good health; in Dutch sensibilities health included cleanliness.

Lastly, houses were expressions of less obvious needs having to do with residents' personal, social, and cultural identity. Being Dutch was important to these descendants of the fatherland even though, and partially because of, being under the control of a British government for most of the colonial period. The Dutch expressed their claims for identity most obviously in their opposition to British ways, at least initially (and in the more remote areas for a longer period). The persistence of the Dutch house can be attributed more to this need than to any other single practical requirement.

Things the Dutch placed in their houses can also be construed as having "needs." If they had a crop of wheat, it had to be stored properly in winter so that mice could not get at it. The garret of the house was more secure than the barn for this purpose, especially to store the seeds on which the next harvest depended. In the eyes of the Dutch their slaves were also possessions akin to their livestock. But like themselves, slaves required similar provisions for security, protection, comfort, and convenience to live healthfully and function productively. The same types of needs, though on a different level, applied to domestic stock (cattle, horses, sheep, pigs, chickens, and so on). Besides wheat and other grains put in garret storage, other crops like potatoes, corn, beans, and peas needed to be processed and stored inside, often in the cellar where there was temperature and moisture regulation as well as security from vermin. Against the latter, dogs and cats were useful. For crops, a root cellar had to be constructed so as to take advantage of the natural warmth of the ground in winter (fifty-two degrees) combined with enough cold from the air above (often below freezing) to maintain an optimum preserving temperature, around forty degrees. In summer, the natural coolness of the cellar helped preserve fresh products such as milk. An occasional Dutch house has been found in which a natural small stream of water was encouraged to run through the cellar year around, moderating temperature to good effect as well as supplying cool, clean water throughout the year.

In Dutch houses a wide range of furnishings provided for the comfort and convenience of residents. Mostly portable, these structures like chests, were used as containers, while chairs and beds provided support for people. Some furnishings, such as ornamental objects, prints, and paintings served identity rather than functional needs. They existed to reassure residents and remind visitors of who they were: Dutch, Protestant, influential, and prosperous (or not, as the case might be). A wide range of utensils—objects used to preserve, prepare, and serve foods—were found in the kitchen, as well as other places in the home. Some were plain utilitarian pieces but others were decorative—they were a convenience to use but also a delight to see

displayed in cupboards or on walls. There were all manner of tools which served to make things or process materials for preserving the structures, feeding mouths, clothing backs, and working the land (if on a farm). All of these possessions needed to be kept secure and maintained. Each had its proper place in the home, barn, or work shed. Knowledge of the range of material objects once owned by the Dutch helps to explain the variety of structures and spaces the Dutch built.

Reading the House

All these requirements of structures, people, animals, crops, and furnishings prompt the question, "How does the house accommodate these needs?" Looking at house features from a functional perspective takes some re-adjustment of mind, since a feature is usually responded to by the eye, not the mind. It takes the mind to ask questions about function, that is, to "read" a house and its evolution. As an example, on a house roof there is a chimney whose purpose is to emit hearth smoke and sparks from inside the house to the outside for the health, safety, and comfort of residents. Why is this important? The hearth fire provides heat for cooking (in the kitchen) and for comfort at other times in winter. A fire creates smoke that can settle as fine ash on anything if it is not disposed of efficiently. This may result in the soiling of furnishings (especially expensive and hard-to-clean fabrics), difficulty breathing, and a fire hazard from sparks. The Dutch had almost no means of protection against destruction by fire which could consume years of hard work and much of their wealth. From a Dutch open hearth, a large funnel-shaped chimney was needed to catch and dispose of smoke and sparks. Such a large chimney was very heavy, being made of bricks, and required massive beams for it to rest on (a second reason for massiveness was to secure a rigid joint to the wall posts against wind pressure). The taller the roof, the taller and heavier the chimney (p. 123), making it more subject to cracking should the roof shift in the wind. Therefore the roof had to be heavily built and braced. Furthermore, the chimney needed to exit at the top or apex of the roof. If it exited down the slope, rainwater and snow from above would run down hard against it causing leaking

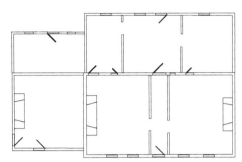

D7 Pieter Claessen Wyckoff House, Brooklyn, NY.

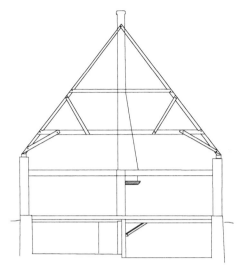

D10 Jean Hasbrouck House, New Paltz, NY.

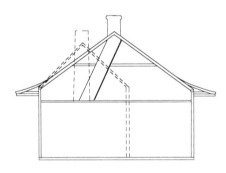

D8 Pieter Claessen Wyckoff House, Brooklyn, NY.

D11 Elevation, Rensselaer Nicoll House, Bethlehem, NY.

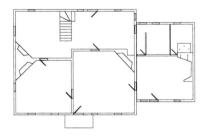

D9 Holmes-Hendrickson House, Holmdel, NJ.

Garrett, left side, Rensselaer Nicoll House, Bethlehem, NY.

and degrading of the mortar joint, and threatening further leaks or a hole from which sparks could start a fire. This was especially so on steep-pitch roofs, the type the Dutch habitually built.

When the Dutch built one-room-deep houses, the fireplace was usually placed on the gable end wall (or sometimes on a central interior partition) and the chimney rose straight to the apex of the roof. But when houses evolved to two-rooms deep, fireplaces in the front or rear room, if in their normal mid-wall position, were not aligned with the apex. The deeper the house, the more unaligned they were. This fact had dramatic consequences. If a house was made deeper by an extra room, the rear rafters could be lifted and extended, leaving the apex and chimney of the front room aligned. If a house was deepened and the roof rebuilt to have a centered apex, then chimneys had to be built at an angle to come ("creep") to the apex (D7, D8) Another solution was to place a front-room fireplace in the back corner of the room, angling it to face the center of the room (D9) This was a Swedish solution adopted by the Dutch in parts of New Jersey (p. 215, p. 210) and placed the chimney at or near the apex of the roof. Back-to-back corner fireplaces with a single chimney could then be accommodated in paired front and back rooms, a feature of a number of New Jersey houses.

Once houses become two rooms deep they usually required a different roof system to avoid the dilemma seen in the Jean Hasbrouck House (p. 123): The roof on this house had to have a very high pitch in order to span its depth. This required massive and closely placed rafters and braces just to secure the roof against wind pressure, a most impractical solution (D10). Such houses were better served by a strong but lower roof structural system that the gambrel roof could provide (D11, *left*). It was lower in total height than Dutch pitch roofs yet did not diminish headroom on the second floor. Being lower it could be constructed of lighter materials with less bracing than a high-pitch roof. Its lower height was dependent on the acceptability of a low-pitch roof and that meant the use of shingles, not tiles or thatch. The gentle slant of the upper roof apparently reduced the

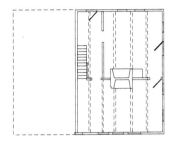

D12 Jacob Adriance House, Queens, NY.

problem of chimney placement below the apex because, for the first time, houses that were two-rooms deep were built with four chimneys, all exiting below the apex in this upper roof slant (p. 205). This helped solve two problems: it reduced run-off weathering of the chimney and improved chimney drafts since, even though not near the apex, the chimney top was not below it.

The new flexibility in chimney placement permitted additional fireplaces in various positions within different rooms making possible the further development of the New Style house. For example, the largest houses of two-rooms deep could take advantage of this depth to build back-to-back fireplaces on interior walls (D12) (p. 198–199). This had the double advantage of allowing four fireplaces (eight, if one includes second-floor rooms, and more if there were cellar fireplaces) with just two chimneys, both exiting at the apex of the roof. One of the largest gambrel roof houses, Historic Cherry Hill in Albany, New York (1786), manages to exit ten fireplaces through two chimneys at the apex of its gambrel roof.

The gambrel roof was a major innovation in New York and New Jersey houses. It was likely borrowed from New Englanders although it is known that a similar (mansard) roof was used in France in medieval times and became popular there after 1650. It could be constructed on the same rafter- and collar-beam structure of the older Dutch houses (rafters above the collar beams being, in effect, cut and lowered to a gentler angle) (p. 40). This evolution worked well

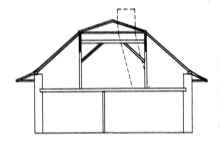

D13 New Jersey gambrel roof structure roof elevation, Roeloff Westervelt House. Tenefly, NJ.

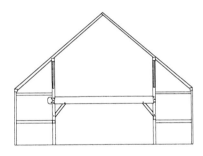

D14 Greater Wemp Barn, Feura Bush, NY.

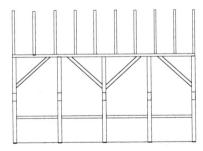

D15 Greater Wemp Barn, Feura Bush, NY.

D16 Jacob Lansing House, Albany, NY.

on shallow one- or one-and-a-half-room-deep gambrel-roof houses, but on deeper houses, around thirty-two- to thirty-four-feet-deep, it was sometimes considered too much of a span for it to handle, so a different but familiar system was used. The Roeloff Westervelt house's gambrel roof (D13) (p. 225) is thirty-four-feet deep and is held up by a relatively light system of posts, braces, and purlins, much like Dutch three-aisle barns (D14, D15) (p. 108). Just the simple question of where a chimney could come out of a roof leads to understanding major changes in the type of roof and even the type of house the Dutch built.

The next question was whether it was necessary to place the fireplace where the Dutch did. Why were most Dutch houses built primarily with fireplaces in the gable end of the house and not in a side wall or on an interior partition? The answer has to do with several requirements to make this type of fireplace useful and efficient. For instance, an important need for the Dutch was to be able to see what they were cooking on the hearth. In a time when candles were expensive, the use of sunlight was heavily depended upon. The best light came from a close-by window which shown light across the hearth from an adjacent wall. This could be accomplished by placing the fireplace on the gable wall and having a window positioned on the side wall nearby (p. 52). It could also be accomplished by placing a fireplace in the middle of the house on a center partition wall opposite a gable-end window. Again, a side-wall window or two could shine outside light across the hearth. The advantage of this position is that it allowed back-to-back fireplaces in rooms sharing a single chimney as in the Leendert Bronck and Pieter Winnie houses (D6) (p. 60, p. 75).

The relative position of the fireplace and its associated window was important in determining the orientation of rural Dutch houses because exterior windows and doors were placed on side walls, making these walls the front and back of the house. Why not reverse this positioning by placing a fireplace on the side wall and windows in the gable end? The Dutch avoided this choice whenever they could because it would place the chimney on the lower part of the roof; it was then subject to much rain and snow run-off damage and poor draft up the chimney. In cities like Albany, however, where gable ends faced the street, fireplaces were sometimes placed in side walls to catch the light of the only windows they had, which were in the gable ends (D16). When done this way, the chimney was subject to much run-off and also had to be built as high as the roof to improve smoke draft, resulting in precariously tall (and exposed) chimney stacks. On the other hand, if set inside the house on the gable wall, a chimney stack kept warm and thus helped draft the smoke more efficiently. An inside chimney also radiated heat within the structure instead of wasting it to the outside. Such a protected chimney also needed far less maintenance since most of it was under the roof.

The need for light for cooking and the need for warmth determined the placement of fireplaces as well as the orientation of the house, but these needs had other consequences. It took much family labor (primarily by slaves in affluent homes) to cut and haul all the firewood needed through the winter and to cook food throughout the year. This made the Dutch cognizant of the need for heating efficiency and the requirement to do whatever was necessary to conserve heat. One consequence of this was that in Dutch houses residents lived compactly, close to the kitchen fireplace; they lived on the first floor only and usually in the kitchen which contained beds, tables, and chairs. A second consequence was that in early Dutch houses, before the advent of the center hall and its open stairway, access to the garret was in the same room as the fireplace. Unless enclosed by a door and partition wall, that stairway could act as a funnel for upward-flowing room heat, wasted in the unused garret. The Teunise Slingerland House is one of the few to retain its original enclosed stairway (p. 88). The subsequent solution to this problem was the center hall, which allowed open access to the garret without wasting heat from a fireplace that was in the same room as the stairway.

Besides the location of the fireplace, its construction affected how the house worked. The traditional Dutch fireplace had evolved over centuries from a "campfire" in the center of the dirt floor. Without a chimney, the smoke accumulated like a head-high cloud under the thatched roof, slowly seeping out. This may have kept the flies away but it made for constant health problems. In time, the hearth was moved to the wall and only later was the chimney developed as a more efficient way to dispose of the smoke, but it required a chimney as wide as a giant upside-down funnel to catch the smoke. The smoke tended to do the same thing it had under the roof— float at head height inside the chimney. Opening a door or window tended to disturb the quiet equilibrium, bringing some of the smoke into the room. Keeping all doors and windows tightly shut was impractical as people came in and out. Such air-tightness also stifled the very need for air flow to encourage the smoke to rise. One solution would have been to lower the chimney frame below head height, but that would certainly have meant constant head injury. Instead the Dutch hung a cloth valance around the opening and with that was born the final form of the Dutch open fireplace, both in The Netherlands and in the New World.

Visitors to New York, unacquainted with this type of fireplace, remarked on its odd appearance. It looked like a fire against the room wall (p. 64). Most examples had no hint of sides of the type found in England, and unless you walked up close and looked upward, you did not notice that there was a chimney, although in fact it was huge (p. 123). It was built upon the heavy beam framework of the ceiling, that is, upon a deep fireplace beam and two transverse beams which formed a rectangular frame linked to the wall.

For various reasons, this ancient medieval form was favored by the Dutch to the exclusion of any other fireplace type. Despite the large brick chimney it was much lighter in weight than a jambed fireplace, an essential consideration in the home country where so many houses were built on, in effect, peat bogs. Those houses were held up by tree trunks driven into the soil by the dozens, a costly but essential foundation. Houses were built of all-wood frames (although often surrounded by a thin wall of brick for fire protection and elegance) because they were light in weight, and fireplaces had to be as light as possible.

Without forests, the Dutch had to rely on dried peat for fuel, and an open, well drafted fireplace served well for this fuel which needed a lot of air to make it burn properly. A funnel chimney which sucked up a lot of air was fine for this purpose even though it created uncomfortable drafts. The Dutch felt is was better to deal with cold than smoke. On the other hand, there were advantages to the Dutch fireplace. Housewives appreciated the wide-open expansiveness of their fireplaces and that they could have multiple small fires going simultaneously. Several trammels could hang down from the large chimney and hold pots at different heights and locations. When the family sat down to eat, the open fireplace gave off lots of light to all corners of the room, creating a pleasant ambiance often remarked on by modern-day observers who have never experienced this type of fireplace. The Dutch fireplace has charm, not just associated with its novelty but because of the visual, even romantic, qualities of its fire light.

When the Dutch came to America they could have changed how they built their houses and fireplaces. They had no worries about soft ground, light construction, and smoking peat fuel. They readily adopted stone as a building material, yet they clung to their old-style fireplaces no matter how much cold draft they caused and how much smoke blew into the room and settled as ash on possessions. Dutch housewives were understandably compulsive about cleaning since their fireplaces were built-in soot machines. Yet for one hundred fifty years many Dutch persisted in ignoring the benefits of English jambed fireplaces. It was only when the Dutch reluctantly embraced English ideas in general that they transformed their fireplaces into the English style; the fireplace conversion was complete by the time of the Revolution. Functionally, the smaller English fireplace had advantages: it burned wood more efficiently, with less draft; its weight-supporting jambs made possible the construction of a fireplace on the floor above which enabled upstairs bedrooms to be heated (D11, p. 104–105); and it created alcoves on either side which were turned into cupboards, a storage feature unknown in Dutch houses up to that time. The cupboards allowed carpenters to create elegant archi-

1750s Fireplace wall, Pieter Winnie House, Bethlehem, NY.

tectural paneling across the fireplace wall, lending a new decorative style to homes (p. 104-105).

Regulating temperature extended to other features besides the form of the fireplace. When iron stoves were introduced (some houses had them as early as the 1720s in the upper Hudson River Valley), they produced convection heat, warming the air in a room quickly with much less wood and with far less heat going up the chimney pipe. They were more efficient, yet the Dutch adopted them slowly in most regions. We occasionally find evidence of the use of five-plate stoves which were set against the wall of one room and fed wood through a hole in the wall from a fireplace in the adjoining room (and exited its smoke back through the hole into the fireplace chimney) (p. 128). This highly efficient convenience heated the "stove room" without losing any heat up a pipe or chimney in that room.

In the back of each fireplace was once found a cast iron fireback (*see above*). Most people assume their purpose was to radiate heat into the room, like a modern radiator. In fact it did nothing of the sort as nearly all convection heat (heated air) generated by the fire, including heat given off by a hot fireback, went up the stack immediately. The purpose of the fireback was to protect the wall from the effects of that heat which in one winter of constant burning can burn out bricks and even stone. An open fire merely radiates heat (as the sun does) warming people and objects but not the air directly, although warmed objects and walls do subsequently give off convection heat. Open fireplaces, therefore, take a long time to warm a cold room but require less fuel to maintain warmth thereafter, especially after the walls have become heated. Walls were, in effect, a heat sink helping to moderate changes in temperature from the inside or the outside. One of the advantages of brick and stone walls was their ability to hold heat through the night when a fire burned out, moderating the night-cooling effect that people in wooden houses were subjected to.

Brick and stone walls had the added advantage of being wind-tight, keeping out the cold blast of winter. Where means and materials were available, the Dutch preferred the use of brick and stone for these heat-saving reasons, but also for its attractiveness, durability, and fire resistance. Houses with overlapping, but not tight, weatherboards had to be made wind-tight by additional measures. Filling the walls with brick nogging (cheap bricks set in clay) or wattle and daub (usually sticks and straw, and plaster) made houses more wind-tight, and the filling acted as a heat sink. However, this fill was never as tight as stone or brick houses.

Doors and windows were important for regulating temperature in all seasons. Hinged window casements and the upper half of exterior doors could be opened for cooling and to bring in light during the summer. Windows had shutters which were closed most of the winter for insulation against the cold; the fireplace window was not shuttered so as to allow light inside. Shutters were closed in summer to insulate against the heat of the day—either from the exterior warm air or the direct rays of the sun. One casement window and shutter in the Van Zandt house in Albany (p. 10) was kept closed so much of the time that someone cut a small hole in it with its own small "shutter" to allow quick looks outside without having to open the shutter.

Kitchen /Slave House, Exterior, Mabee Farm, Rotterdam Junction, NY.

The need to regulate summer temperature was one motivation for the typical Dutch improvement of adding a "summer" kitchen. A cooking fireplace burning in the hot days of summer was likely a sufficient inducement for moving the cooking to a separate hearth away from the main family room. Evolving designs included adding a kitchen wing, building a separate "out"-kitchen, having another kitchen in the cellar, or, for those already living in small one-room houses, building an attached or separate main house with more rooms, making it possible to convert the original room into the extra kitchen. Likewise, brick bake ovens were built either into the back of Dutch fireplaces (projecting out of the back wall of the gable, p. 136) or as separate free-standing ovens outside of the house. The former was convenient, the later was more comfortable. Kitchen houses also served as residences, at least in summer, for any servants and slaves. The one-room kitchen house at the Mabee Farm (*above*) is relatively unchanged from its original state, providing evidence of work and habitation there.

Another method of regulating heat was devised in the southern parts of New York and New Jersey. Extended eaves, also called "bell-cast" or spring eaves, after the gracefully curved outward extension of the roof line over the walls, are

Exterior, Left Gable End Width, The Joseph Guyon House, Historic Richmond Town, NY.

extended eaves, even to double eaves, one for each floor level, sharing some of the same functions, if not same structure, as those on Dutch houses.

Extended eaves proved to have a long-lasting appeal, more so than nearly any other early architectural feature in New Jersey and New York, suggesting there were ingrained beliefs about its function. The closest structural analogy to the extended eaves is the pentice, an especially New York Dutch feature which is a small roof or porch over an exterior door (p. 78). The pentice was built on houses and on the main wagon doors of Dutch barns. Its function was to shed rainwater away from the front door and the stoop in front of it, thereby helping to preserve them from excessive water and rot. This feature was especially prevalent over the large wagon doors of Dutch barns (p. 120) that had a "stoop" consisting of wood ramps rising up over the sill and into the barn flooring. Without the pentice, these would have been exposed to the elements.

acknowledged as one of the most attractive aspects of early houses in this region (D13)(p. 193, p. 205, p. 214). Extended eaves are to be found almost exclusively on one-and-a-half story houses, not on full two-story houses (The Voorlezer's House (p. 203) is an unusual exception, because of habitation on the second floor). They are mostly on the front facade (usually with a southerly exposure) and less frequently on rear facades. They extend from a few inches to five feet from the wall. Some were included at the same time the house was built; others were added later. They continued to be incorporated into new houses built throughout the eighteenth and well into the nineteenth centuries (some were included as early as the seventeenth century).

Such eaves occur primarily in the southern parts of New York and in New Jersey, areas settled by Dutch and other nationalities including Huguenots, the Protestant refugees from Catholic France. Similar eaves are found in houses in northwest France and in Quebec Canada, suggesting the idea came to the New World through French immigrants. They were not a feature used on New England houses, but German houses in the Delaware Valley have analogous

The function of the pentice led some to assume that the extended eaves on other houses were primarily for keeping rainwater away from the front of a house, protecting the siding, shutters, windows, doorways, stoop, and foundation from this source of rot. No doubt extended eaves gave protection to the side walls of a house, a useful measure in parts of Europe where whitewashed plaster exterior walls were subject to weathering. But such siding was not used in the colonies and the survival of weatherboard, brick, and stone houses testifies to the fact that such an overhang was not necessary. But even if siding is secure enough from the weather, it is not necessarily the case that other features of a house such as shutters, door and window sills, stoops, and cellars are free of weather problems. Recent experience has shown that all these are subject to rot from exposure. Indeed no original stoop is known to have survived into the twentieth century. Furthermore, photographs and illustrations of Dutch houses dating from the prior century rarely, if ever, suggest an original stoop even in that period. Extended eaves diminished, if not eliminated, such exposure to weather. In addition, canted doors (hatchways) over cellar entrances are to be found next to

*At the back of the large house [The Schuyler Flatts]
was a smaller and lower one, . . . [it] afforded a refuge
to the family during the rigors of winter, when the
spacious summer rooms would have been intolerably
cold, and the smoke of prodigious wood fires would have
sullied the elegantly clean furniture. Here, too, was
a sunk story, where the kitchen was immediately below
the eating parlor. . . .* —Anne Grant, Albany,
1756–63 [Memoirs, I: 170–1]

Front Exterior, The Arriantje and Samuel Coeymans House,
Coeymans, NY.

front doors on many Long Island Dutch houses. Like shutters and window and door sills, they too rot from exposure, perhaps less so where they get partial protection from extended eaves.

Such an overhang is not to be seen in the upper Hudson River Valley. There may be practical reasons for its non-adoption there. Winters in the north are more severe, on average as much as twenty degrees colder than in New Jersey. That allows snow to accumulate, creating occasionally heavy snow loads on roofs. Houses with steep roofs, so characteristic of the Albany area, cope with these loads easily. Houses with lower pitch roofs cope less well. In the colder northern region the melt and re-thaw of day and night creates ice dams causing melting snow to back up as water under shingles and leak inside a house. Extended eaves would not only be threatened by the excessive weight of heavy snow loads but would be ideally shaped to create ice dams that increase the weight on the eaves even more than snow. The warmer climate of the southern region has largely avoided these problems.

In order to make a tight seal at the roof line, the distinctive extended eave roof must be of moderate or low pitch if it is to curve into the eave without a sharp break. The Dutch had always preferred a steep roof, as on the Luykas Van Alen house (p. 63), for it shed rain more efficiently, especially when materials such as tile or thatch were used. In the New World, however, they soon adapted wood shingles for roofing which allowed for a lower yet weather-tight roof and this made possible gradually sloping roofs with graceful extended eaves. In New York and other cities where fireproof roofing was desired, the use of tiles for this purpose necessitated steep roofs long after they were deemed unnecessary on shingled rural houses. Thus we see what would appear to be an historical anomaly but practical necessity—the persistence of old-style Netherlands houses in New York City even though this city was the most progressive center for new house ideas in the colony. The innovation of building lower roofs and extended eaves was adopted first in the countryside and Long Island. From there it spread across New York harbor to Staten Island and into New Jersey.

Extended eaves were also useful as shelter in other ways. The amount of externally produced cold and heat entering the home was moderated with shutters, as previously discussed. An overhanging roof, if it extended outward far enough, could serve the same function as shutters: extended eaves could shade windows from direct sunlight during the hot summer days when the sun was high in the sky, making it unnecessary to adjust shutters daily; in winter, when the sun was lower in the sky, extended eaves could shine light into windows when warmth was desired.

In better houses, there was a concern that direct sunlight was deleterious to valuable fabrics, especially curtains. In Georgian and Federal houses interior as well as exterior shutters were used for sheltering fabrics and furniture, and increasing personal comfort by controlling temperature. Nineteenth-century exterior shutters were more often louvered than solid panel, reflecting the fact that with more efficient heating systems, such as cast iron stoves, solid shutters were not necessary for insulation. Regardless of outside air temperature, venti-

Exterior, Holmes Hendrickson House, Holmdel, NJ.

lation was desirable while still controlling direct sunlight, and louvered shutters served these functions well.

Some eaves were extended so far that they were supported by posts (p. 205) thus creating, in effect, the porch (or piazza, as it was called in those days). This distinctly American addition to nineteenth-century houses functioned as an extended eave but provided benefits to people as well as the structure. The solar heating and cooling properties of extended eaves are still recognized in contemporary structures such as ranch houses and their academic antecedent, Frank Lloyd Wright's prairie houses.

Room Evolution

How and why rooms were increased in number and size and altered in arrangement is paramount to understanding the evolution of the Dutch house. The need to use rooms for specific human functions became the engine that drove major changes in the lifestyles of the Dutch and, consequently, changes in their houses. Changes in rooms—from the earliest one-room pioneer Dutch houses to the fully

developed, large center-hall Georgian mansions—is directly attributable to improvements in resources, wealth, and a new way of living.

The first innovation was the expansion of the one-room pioneer house into two rooms, and then its further expansion by adding a separate or attached kitchen wing. This is clearly seen in early Long Island houses, however its prevalence elsewhere in New York and New Jersey suggests it was a Dutch, not an English, idea. This expression reveals a desire for functional differentiation, providing increased room as the family increased in size and added servants and slaves. It also contributed to overall privacy and comfort among these residents.

The pioneer house was small, often just one room because of the necessity of quickly establishing shelter on a new farm. Such was the case when Pieter Bronck built his house on a remote frontier site in New York, now Coxsackie, in 1663 (p. 56). Similar early houses were also small because of the owners' poverty or lack of industry. Given their age, modesty, and quick construction, few survive. Sometime after initial construction, however, most such houses were added to in one of a number of possible ways: an identical room was attached to the one-room house providing the family with a parlor (best room or *groote kamer*) in addition to the kitchen; a smaller addition was attached to one gable end of a larger house to create a kitchen (p. 215); a large two-room addition, set perpendicular to or in line with the original one-room house, could be built and these rooms became the parlor and main kitchen, while the original room became the summer kitchen (p. 225); and, finally, a house that already had two rooms was added to with one or more rooms. In these houses, the additional room was placed off to the side like an L and used as a second kitchen (p. 55) or could be placed as a room or as a hall and room off the gable end to create the extra kitchen (p. 63). As discussed previously, a separate summer or out kitchen could be built near the main house.

The principal motivation behind these changes was to create a separate habitation space for greater comfort in the hot summer and for greater privacy from servants and slaves. In Bergen County, parents often retired to these sections when the younger son and his family took over the main house.

Thus the Dutch house expanded in various ways yet retained its essential character and features. Given enough wealth, it was adaptable to expanding family size and to greater requirements for comfort and convenience. Yet despite all these changes, the Dutch house retained its basic room functions for a long time. Special occasions were held in—and valuable possessions placed in—the *groote kamer*, but its fireplace was seldom used because the room was seldom used and because the Dutch were mindful of the dirt it would deposit on their treasured objects.

The adjacent family kitchen was the location for nearly all work, socializing, and sleeping. A second kitchen, or summer kitchen, as has been described, whether attached or separate, was used as such and as servants and slave quarters. In winter, however, with conservation of heat more important, the main-house kitchen became the center of living and cooking, at least for the family. In some places, this arrangement was a part of newly constructed Dutch-style houses well into the nineteenth century.

All of the above house configurations were of one room depth in the medieval form which allowed little privacy and protection from the elements. The subsequent evolution of the Dutch house was driven by a desire for a more modern and affluent style of home life emphasizing greater privacy and comfort, although not as yet quite the acceptance of the New Style life. These changes were incorporated into house designs in all areas—earliest near New York City and much later in the upper Hudson River Valley. These owe more to English cultural innovations than to anything else, such as the differentiation of household functions which created a need for more rooms which in turn necessitated the adoption of the central hall which allowed for two rooms on either side. This led to adopting the New England use of the gambrel roof which allowed for deeper houses yet provided

more headroom on the second floor where bedrooms and fireplaces were now being installed.

One of the first changes away from the Dutch tradition was the insertion of a hall. The addition to the Van Alen House, c. 1750 (p. 63), provided a hallway between two rooms. For the first time, a public entryway separate from the rooms was created, insulating them from outside temperature and wind while introducing greater privacy and increased comfort in the house. The next accommodation, often adopted before the hall, was to change the Dutch fireplace into the jambed English-style fireplace, as previously discussed. This was easily done by incorporating the new fireplace under the Dutch hood chimney. To some people, this change may have merely been a practical move towards greater efficiency and comfort as English fireplaces required less fuel and provided more heat, and also allowed greater control over smoke and consequent soiling in the room. To others, however, a conversion to the use of English-style fireplaces was the harbinger of the Dutch acceptance of the New Style, with all the implications that it held for future changes throughout the house.

Additional alterations associated with the newer style can be seen in the expansion of rooms into a number of configurations. For example, some early Dutch houses were built with a room and a half (chamber and antechamber), with the second room to the rear and not to the side. This rear, smaller room was primarily used as a bedroom separate from the main room, the beginning of greater privacy. Most half-size back rooms or antechambers did not have fireplaces; the Dutch did not consider it an inconvenience if a sleeping area was unheated. One still frequently finds Dutch bed warmers in antique shops, a testament to their popularity and necessity for warming cold beds in these unheated back rooms (note that most date from the first half of the nineteenth century). Bed warmers are associated with the curtained tester bed and the enclosed cupboard bed by which one could keep a modicum of all-night warmth merely from one's own body heat within the enclosed space. The Roeloff Westervelt House in Tenafly, New Jersey, bears evidence of another kind of curtained bed. In the two large front rooms and the two antechambers behind are wrought-iron eyelets in the ceiling forming bed-sized corners, likely an economical way of hanging curtains on the two exposed sides of each bed corner. No doubt such enclosed beds also served the purpose of increasing privacy in rooms inhabited by many people.

Another type of room expansion was created by doubling the size of a one-and-a-half-room house so that two large rooms were in front and two or more smaller rooms were in back, as in the Hendrickson House (p. 215) in Monmouth County, New Jersey (D9). This house type had one or two front doors and usually one rear door. The rear entrance was used in winter so that the small back room could act as a hallway insulating the main fireplace rooms from the cold. It was a disadvantage to have a front door opened when a fire was burning in the same room, since it could cause smoke to come out into the room if there was any wind outside. A second disadvantage was that the cold blast chilled residents in the room and required more fire to reheat the room. Both concerns became strong inducements to adopt the English center hall.

But why a separate door to each room in the first place? Early Dutch houses, as well as some later ones, were constructed with two front rooms each with an outside entry door (p. 63). This configuration was not found in The Netherlands where farmhouses, if separate from barns as in America, are found in parts of the provinces of Friesland and Zeeland. They are configured quite differently from American examples and so do not have paired rooms with paired entrances. Some authorities assert that it can be found in Flanders (Belgium) and northern France, arguing that the idea was brought by the Huguenots to New York and New Jersey (and by Catholic French to Quebec).

Historical precedent, while informative, is not enough to justify adoption of a feature without functional utility. If one looks at function before form, the usefulness of double entries is not such a mystery. Given the main purpose of the *groote kamer* as a space primarily for formal social occasions, a separate exterior entrance was appropriate rather than having guests pass through a crowded kitchen. In addition, when the *groote kamer* was in use the temperature in the kitchen was easier to maintain if firewood and people were brought through its own exterior door.

Not all houses with two rooms and no center hall had exterior doors for both rooms. Bethlehem House (p. 98) originally had four rooms: on the left side there was a small room in the front with an exterior door, as well as a large fireplace room behind it; this room also gave entry to a large room on the right side which also had a small room behind it. The small entry room acted as a hallway controlling access to, and keeping the outside elements from, the two main rooms. This small room also contained the stairway and thus controlled any loss of heat upstairs. Such a building arrangement was a way of receiving the benefit of a central hall without the extra expense of a wider house. It also provided public access to what had been, up to that point, the open garret, a mostly uninhabited area. In this house the full second story was composed of bedrooms from the beginning.

The development of upstairs bedrooms introduced the opportunity for a new use for the second floor in these houses. In earlier Dutch houses living areas existed only on the first floor or, in some cases, the cellar fireplace room, unless owners built a special structure like the Voorlezer's House (p. 202), where the upstairs was a residence and the downstairs was used for business. The newer style required separate bedrooms and this resulted in utilizing the second floor for this purpose. At first, one bedroom was placed upstairs, a major departure from a centuries-old medieval tradition of living only on the main floor. Later, two bedrooms were created.

With the adoption of second-floor bedrooms, the Dutch also adopted the idea of fireplaces in those bedrooms, but this required a major structural change. The Dutch fireplace with its hood chimney resting on ceiling beams could not support, much less accommodate, a fireplace in the garret above. A Dutch fireplace could be built above another only if there was an additional set of heavy beams on the second level. This was accomplished in the Arriantje Coeymans House in 1717–18 (p. 79) because it was a rare two-story Dutch house. But in more typical one-and-a-half-story-high Dutch houses, there was no way to support a fireplace on the second floor, be it Dutch or English. The only option was to build a strong jambed fireplace on the first floor which could support both a chimney and a smaller jambed fireplace with its own flue next to the fireplace on the second floor (D11) (p. 98). It can be argued that the placement of bedrooms on the second floor created a structural imperative to adopt the English jambed fireplace in Dutch houses regardless of any preference for the newer style or greater efficiency.

The New Style House

Once the two major structural-functional problems—the roof and its chimney placement, and the placement of second-floor fireplaces—were solved, the fully developed Georgian house superseded the old-style Dutch house in most areas. Not at the same time (the upper Hudson River Valley was always more conservative), and not uniformly within any area, but among the more affluent merchants, landowners, and farmers it was the style of choice, especially after 1750. Of course, it took more money to build these houses. It also took more to run them. More fireplaces meant more firewood, and therefore more servants, food, crops, and land. Like houses, farmers and traders were evolving, finally accepting the English style of living, including its emphasis on wealth tied to class consciousness.

We now come to the final development of the colonial house type in this former Dutch colony—the newer style home with a central hall and one or two rooms on either side, and a stairway within the hall leading to bedrooms on the second floor. The central hall became the buffer between public and private rooms and between outside elements and inside comfort. Once the front and rear doors entered a hall there was no longer a necessity for the stairway to be enclosed. It now became an elegant and graceful feature of the center hall, a statement of the social importance of the house and its

owner. Upstairs bedrooms accessed only from the hall meant real privacy for the first time. That was what the newer style life and house was about. Houses became expressions of class and group status and socializing became a means to express acceptance into that society. Decorative features such as higher ceilings and more luxurious furnishings were incorporated into houses to express and confirm achievement. In large houses there was a division between private (family) and public spaces, usually with the real or implied divide across the center hall: the rear area was used for the family with a rear sitting and dining room below and bedrooms above. The family rooms were simpler, contrasting with the elegance lavished on the front, or public, rooms which consisted of a dining room and parlor and large bedrooms above. The major change in these homes was an expression of a change in society correlating with the acceptance of English social norms—class distinctions expressed through taste and wealth lavished on the design of the house and its social use.

The Homes

The Luykas Van Alen House
Kinderhook, Columbia County, New York

The word kitchen (*kuken*) does not express
the multiple purposes of this Dutch room
for it served as the central area of living—
cooking, dining, sleeping, and socializing all
in one place. With many children it would
appear to us more like camping than living,
but that is how people in the medieval
tradition lived. It was not until the 1760s
in the more conservative upriver region
that English influence changed living
arrangements and room functions, creating
separate bedrooms on the second floor.

*"The fire places have no Jambs (as ours have)
But the Backs run flush with the walls, and the
Hearth is of tyles and farr out into the room at
the ends as before the fire, which is Generally
Five foot in the Low'r rooms, and the piece over
where the mantle tree should be is made as ours
with Joyners work, and as I supose fasten'd to
iron rodds inside."* —Madame Sarah Knight,
New York City, 1704 [*Private Journal,*
pp. 52–3]

The Northern Frontier

The Mohawk and Upper Hudson River Valleys

Old Albany County

Old Albany County was the region of the upper Hudson River Valley surrounding the city of Albany. Since the Revolutionary War it has consisted of Albany, Schenectady, Rensselaer, Greene, and Columbia Counties. For all of its colonial existence the greater Albany County was the northern frontier of the colony. It drew settlers in the beginning because it afforded close access to fur trading with the Native Americans. In subsequent years its fertile river plains encouraged extensive farming. Fort Orange (built in 1624) and its adjacent town (Beverwyck) evolved into the village, and then city of Albany after 1664. This small but bustling outpost was the hub of all commerce, government, and trade relations between Manhattan and Montreal.

Beverwyck (or Albany) was settled early by Dutch traders and families. Its great distance from New Amsterdam (one hundred fifty miles) and dependence on itself for prosperity fostered an independent spirit from the political center of the colony. This attitude was sometimes expressed by a certain arrogance toward outsiders and a disdain for their ways. As late as a century after the English conquest of the colony, the area's Dutch were contemptuous of English visitors and officials. They remained culturally conservative, retaining Dutch customs long after English manners had acculturated into the Dutch populations closer to New York City.

The most obvious outward expression of this attitude can still be seen in their surviving houses. The Albany region retains a type of Dutch brick house that is nearly gone from other regions, if indeed it was ever common elsewhere. A distinctive feature of this house type is the parapet gable of which the Van Alen (p. 63) and Bronck (p. 57) houses are prime examples. They resemble more closely than any surviving American Dutch houses a type found in The Netherlands. Although built two generations after New Netherland became English, these houses betray not a single feature of English influence. They were built for the most prosperous farmers. Urban versions were built in Albany and Schenectady by enterprising merchants and traders.

Other houses were less costly and stylish in construction, befitting the more modest means of tenant farmers and town laborers and shop keepers. These were mostly of wood, that is, sawn weatherboards, both in the two towns and on the farms. On the west side of the Hudson River rural houses were more often made of stone as they were close to a ridge of limestone which runs the entire length of that side of the Hudson River from Albany south to Kingston and then inland to Port Jervis on the Delaware river. The earliest surviving stone house in this region is the pioneer one-room Jonas Bronck house of 1663 (p. 56) at Coxsackie, south of Albany. Stone was not available in The Netherlands in quantity, so using it for walls in the New World was an innovative adaptation by the Dutch, the first major change in building practice. Adapting a new material did not, however, change the basic layout or other details of their homes. These features remained essentially Dutch until the 1760s in the upper Hudson River Valley.

Wood houses were cheaper and much quicker to build and from the outset were the preferred type for these reasons. Like stone, wood was not easily obtained in The Netherlands where it was mostly imported from other nations, primarily to Amsterdam and its surrounding areas. So plentiful was the Albany area in trees that settlers cut and burned them to prepare for planting crops. By the eighteenth century lumber became an important local industry with water powered saw mills on every suitable stream.

The quality of houses built depended not just on materials but on who built the house and where it was built. Much of the Hudson River Valley was granted to a few individuals to establish manors and settle rent-paying tenants. As a result little land was left for freehold purchase. Manorial tenants received the use of a farm but they could not pass its title to their children, a disincentive to building structures better than necessity required. Tenant houses, therefore, were almost all simple wood or stone houses. Wood houses were once plentiful but now scarce, having disappeared from rot or fire. Stone houses have survived quite well.

The manorial system was begun under the Dutch who granted patroonships—large parcels of land with certain rights—to individuals who were then responsible for getting immigrants to settle there. In the upper Hudson River Valley the patroonship of Rensselaerswyck encompassed such a large region around the one early settlement, Albany, that the opportunity to own one's own land was effectively cut off for decades. When the British took the colony they also made many manorial grants but mostly they sold land patents to speculators who could do on a more modest scale what the Van Rensselaers had done, rent land or sell it to individuals. Not surprisingly, the latter opportunity inspired owners to build more impressive houses than tenants did, witness those belonging to Van Alen (p. 63), Bronck (p. 57), and Coeymans (p. 78).

The Pieter Winnie House
Bethlehem Township, Albany County, NY

The stone wing forms an **L** and was undoubtedly intended to be used as a kitchen. Two fireplaces of the open Dutch form were originally built in the cellar and room above, the latter converted to jambed form shortly thereafter and a paneled wall with cupboards installed (but now missing). A 1750s fire back made by the Oxford Furnace of Sussex (now Warren) County, New Jersey, helps date this fireplace conversion.

55

The Bronck Houses

The Pieter Bronck House *(left)*
The Leendert Bronck House *(right)*
Coxsackie, Greene County, New York
Greene County Historical Society, Coxsackie, New York

Pieter Bronck (c.1617–1669) built this house in around
1663. A true pioneer home of just one room, it is the oldest
surviving structure in the Hudson Valley and our guide
to visualizing life in the seventeenth century. Casement
windows, a steep roof, and fieldstone walls represent a time
when Native Americans and wolves were still a challenge
to life and farm stock.

EXTERIOR

The characteristic steep pitch of early
Dutch roofs is primarily a function of
Netherlands roofing material—pantiles and
thatch. Both require a steep roof for different reasons. Pantiles are loosely set upon
each other, allowing wind to drive rain
inside unless set at an angle of about fifty-
six degrees. Thatch will not rot if rain can
run off quickly enough. The raised parapet
gable sealed the pantiles along the gable
eaves from wind and weather. In New
Netherland, even when shingles replaced
pantiles, the parapet gable was continued,
more for ornament than practical function.

The walls were covered with all sorts of drawings and pictures in small frames. On each side of the chimneys they had usually a sort of alcove, and the walls under the windows were wainscoted and had benches placed near them. The cupboards and all the wood work were painted with a bluish gray color. —Peter Kalm, 1749–50 [*Travels*, p. 132]

KITCHEN HOUSE INTERIOR

Although dating from a later period than others in this book, this summer kitchen house is one of the few to survive intact and unchanged. Such separate kitchens were appreciated in the era of open-fire cooking. With the advent of cast iron cooking stoves, the discomfort of radiant heated open fire-places in summer abated and summer kitchens began to take on other uses or were demolished. It was at this same time that the other use for these structures—slave or servant-quarters—began to diminish as slavery was abolished in New York and New Jersey.

THE PIETER BRONCK HOUSE, INTERIOR

Bible-inspired Delftware tiles and a painting reminded the Dutch of their faith and scriptural parallels to their own experiences. In the New World they thought of themselves, in the Biblical sense, as a "remnant in the wilderness," appropriate enough for this frontier house. A later paneled fireplace wall with cupboards (c. 1770) marks the advance of English culture in the Hudson Valley just before the Revolution.

The Leendert Bronck House

The Bronck houses are unique in their additions and configuration. A pioneer one-room stone house (1663) was expanded in 1738 by the next generation; they added a separate two-room brick house that was joined to the original by a passageway. A generation later, a room and hall was added to the back of the original house. And a third generation added a close by but separate kitchen house in 1815. In keeping with this tradition, when a Bronck descendant gave the property in the 1930s to the Greene County Historical Society, he built an adjacent house, of similar form, for a caretaker. Leendert Bronck (b. 1699, m. 1717) was especially conscious of the quality of his new brick house such that he kept it separate from his old house by a covered passageway containing this doorway rather than building onto the old stone house. The same motivation inspired Coeymans to separate her big and smaller houses by a large passageway (p. 79).

INTERIOR,
SOUTH ROOM (*top*),
NORTH ROOM (*bottom*)

The Bronck house interior is best read as a lesson in the changing taste and lifestyle of a Dutch family that was becoming Americanized. While most house museums have been restored to their early period and furnished accordingly, the rarest of house museums are those that are fortunate to have the history of a family made visible by their surviving possessions.

INTERIOR, SOUTH ROOM

The 1738 Bronck house is one of the few remaining fully developed brick Dutch houses of Netherlands style. Both main rooms have exterior doors, the south room containing the stairway to the garret and cellar; most likely both flights were once enclosed. The far door leads to the covered passageway of the early Bronck house. Placing the fireplaces back-to-back on the central partition instead of the gable end walls made possible the placement of the stairway and the passageway door.

The Luykas Van Alen House

Kinderhook, Columbia County, New York
Columbia County Historical Society, Kinderhook, New York

When Luykas Van Alen set out to build his family home in 1737, he had the benefit of inheritance (his father owned 17,000 acres) and a desire to have a substantial house in the old Netherlands style. He built this home in 1737 and shortly after added a hall and room to the right. Each room had an exterior door allowing convenient entry to any room and thereby some privacy to others.

The Van Alen House remained remarkably unchanged throughout its life. In the nineteenth century the original stairway was replaced and partitions were added on both floors to make more rooms. Until received by the Columbia County Historical Society in 1963 no utilities had been installed. Today it is one of the best surviving examples of this distinctively Dutch brick parapet-gable house and is open as a museum.

EXTERIOR

Dutch houses are vertical structures of horizontal use. They have a cellar, a main floor, a garret floor for storage, and often, as in the Van Alen house, an upper garret. Yet habitation was almost exclusively on the main floor, with an occasional cellar kitchen. The larger section is the original house of 1737.

The addition to the right was added shortly thereafter in the same style creating a hall and room, likely a summer kitchen and residence for servants and slaves. The hallway was an innovation at that time, sheltering rooms from direct exposure to the outside, providing comfort and privacy.

Early New York houses were often surrounded by black locust trees (valued for their flowers, among other attributes), descendants of which shade the Van Alen house today.

The Locust Tree (Robinia pseudacasia)
is usually planted near the Houses where
ornament is sought for, on account of the
fragrance of the blossom in summer, the beauty
of the foliage at all times, and an opinion that
it fertilizes the ground which it covers . . .
—William Strickland, 1794–95 [*Journal*, p. 101]

GREAT ROOM (*GROOTE KAMER*) AND FIREPLACE

The main floor of Dutch houses most often has just two rooms, the great room (*groote kamer* in Dutch) or parlor, and the kitchen, most activities being in the latter. The great room with its fine furnishings was reserved for special occasions, although the parents usually slept there.

The open Dutch fireplace (with no sides or jambs) dominates a room by its size and unusual form. Its large funnel-like chimney draws out both smoke and warmth, an inefficiency in winter but a blessing in summer. The open fireplace gives out a wide glow to a room enhancing its social appeal. The New World Dutch continued to use this fireplace long after the smaller English jambed fireplace was known to them; its efficiency less important than their own traditions.

KITCHEN WINDOW

Massive smooth-planed deep beams, high ceilings, large casement windows, and bright colors were thoroughly old fashioned in 1737 but still functional. A strong wooden structure secured with braces (corbels) insures the integrity of the brick walls. High ceilings are imposing but also allow large windows and therefore more light to enter a room.

The windows are high & large, as are the stories, ten or 12 foot ye first, the casements of wood at bottom of the windows, and without, strong and thick shutters. The chimneys without Jawmes, hanging like the Topp of a pulpitt, but usually a good rich fringed callico, or other stuffe halfe a yard deep at ye edges, with Dutch tyles on each side the fire place, carried up very high. They also tyle theyr sides of ye staircase and bottom of windows, they have excellent pictures, and good down bedds . . .
—Dr. Benjamin Bullivant, New York, 1697 [*Travel Diary*, p. 65]

GREAT ROOM (*GROOTE KAMER*) FURNISHINGS

Light was important to the Dutch and this can be seen in their early paintings and in their houses. Large windows admit it and whitewash walls reflect it, all to better see their work and treasures.

The furniture is Hudson Valley, but more English in style than Dutch. This change of cultural preference began with the rich Anglo-Dutch merchants and manor lords who adopted English ways and furnishings in the late seventeenth century, an idea that progressed slowly up river over the next century.

KITCHEN WINDOW

The Dutch were fond of objects which were as pleasing to the eye as to their purpose. Delftware (tin-glazed earthenware) dishes, pewter chargers, brass candlesticks, and earthenware pots were, like their houses, both functional and fascinating. Here they are displayed upon a Hudson River Valley *potte-bank*—pottery shelf—in sunlight which bathes the hearth, the heart of the home. Making sure there was adequate light upon the hearth, where most domestic work was done, has more to do with where windows were positioned in a Dutch house than anything else.

The Cornelis Schermerhorn House

Kinderhook, Columbia County, New York

From its start in the 1660s, Kinderhook was a different place. Sandwiched between the feudal manors of the Van Rensselaers and Livingstons, it was the land of opportunity for freeholders interested in creating estates to pass on to their children. The Van Schaacks, Schermerhorns, Van Alens, and Van Alstynes, among others, created large farms and their children populated them with houses which now form the village.

GARDEN

Formal Dutch gardens found favor in colonial America while the English landscape design was adopted in the United States in the nineteenth century. In both England and the United States, however, the popularity of naturalistic landscaping nearly swept away the formal gardens of the earlier era. Boxwood gardens are only now reasserting their presence as owners of colonial houses rediscover their pleasures outweigh their expense or maintenance.

KNOT GARDEN

European formal gardens of the sixteenth and seventeenth centuries can be seen as outside extensions of interior rooms both in plan (rectilinear) and placement, being close at hand for the pleasure of viewing and wandering within. They were also situated close to the house because they were best viewed from upstairs windows. Beyond the formal gardens the land was left in its natural state of fields and forests.

GREAT ROOM (*GROOTE KAMER*)

Cornelis Schermerhorn's home likely dates
from the time of his marriage in 1713.
At first it was a small structure of a room
and a side hall and a separate kitchen house.
Its great room, like most restored rooms,
provides a look into the past as well as at
present needs and comforts.

GREAT ROOM PAINTING

The Dutch tradition of art came to America
in the seventeenth century, primarily as
imported paintings. Most are lost now, but
what does survive are many portraits and
scripture paintings created here in the early
eighteenth century. Prosperous merchants
and farmers had their faith and features
recorded for posterity by local "limners"
such as Gerardus Duyckinck who painted
this boy's portrait in 1730.

*Their chambers are seldom ceiled; but have
large beams, at the distance of about four feet
asunder, on which the floors are laid. And the
chimneys, which are large, have usually a piece
of scalloped cloth hanging before them, which, at
first sight, gives them the appearance of beds . . .
the houses are both inconvenient and clumsy,
they are kept extremely neat, by constant washing and rubbing.* —Anonymous, Albany, 1789
[*Columbia*, p. 691]

The Albertus Van Loon House

Athens, Greene County, New York

According to a date stone (now covered by road fill) incised "[A?] V L Anno 1724 Ap 2 [?]," the original one-room house is of this date and was built by Albertus Van Loon (1683–1754) of the founding family of Loonenberg, now the village of Athens on the Hudson River. Jan Van Loon, the progenitor of the family in America, was a Lutheran and the community he founded became the upriver center for this sect and the residence of its dominies (ministers). Best remembered is Dominie Berkenymeyer whose carefully documented journal of 1731–50 (*The Albany Protocol*) recreates for us a remarkably intimate view of an early New York community's daily concerns.

In our time, other Dutch houses like this one have gone in and out of habitation, many rescued from a fate most others have suffered. It is hard for us to understand that abandonment need not be permanent—houses can and should be stabilized for use another day. This house recently received just such a reprieve when new owners, sensitive to the qualities others had overlooked, took on a daunting restoration.

CENTER HALL

At first Van Loon's house had but one room, its gable fronting westward on the road and with the river to the east. After the 1750s it was probably expanded on its north side with a center hall, seen here, and second room. The entire house was covered with a realigned new roof in gambrel form.

EXTERIOR

As houses are renovated and neighborhoods developed, the essence of the past diminishes. To recapture it one must focus more closely—on evocative details. The Van Loon house was abandoned for many years yet despite neglect it survives; its craggy gambrel gable intact.

The Pieter Winnie House

Bethlehem Township, Albany County, New York

It is still possible for old houses to be "discovered" anew. This house went unknown to all but local residents until recently when alarm over its deteriorating condition raised concern enough to find a sympathetic new owner who is restoring it with care. The house is in two parts: the first was built by Pieter D. Winnie (born in 1699) about the time he married Rachel Van Alen in 1720; the addition was built in around 1740–50. Although a farm house, the old section is in the urban style of others in nearby Albany, Winnie's birthplace.

FRONT GABLE (C. 1720)

Like an urban Dutch house, its entrance is in a gable end built partially of brick and with a gable in weatherboard slightly overhanging the brick to protect it. The restored steep gable roof and casement windows with leaded sashes follow evidence of the originals. Within are two rooms over a cellar and a garret above. As in other houses of its period and place, both rooms have corbeled bents or H-frames; the ceiling beams and wall posts are exposed. To the left is the stone kitchen addition.

I told him that the time had come to build his house; and for that purpose I would myself invite the neighborhood to a frolic; that thus he would have a large dwelling erected and some upland cleared in one day. . . . About forty people repaired to the spot; the songs and merry stories went round the woods from cluster to cluster, as the people had gathered to their different works; . . . thus the rude house was raised and above two acres of land cut up, cleared, and heaped. . . . Soon after he hired a carpenter, who put on a roof and laid the floors; in a week more, the house was properly plastered and the chimney finished.
—J. Hector St. John de Crevecoeur, Orange County, NY, 1782 [*Letters*, pp. 103–4]

WEATHERBOARD SIDING

The addition's stone wall was simply butted against the weatherboards of the early house, which were remarkably crude in an otherwise finely finished house. Those shown here were left intact to serve as the finished wall in this corner of the addition, which, given the small window, may have been an enclosed alcove off the kitchen. The boards are unusually wide and thick, pit sawn, and merely whitewashed. They are devoid of the smooth planing, beaded edge, and colorful paint otherwise associated with Dutch house siding.

GARRET

Some houses have been so heavily renovated that stripping them back to original material is a reasonable course especially if the renovation lacks any redeeming quality. The Winnie house had been so abused, misused, and then neglected that it was only recently discovered to be an early house. Its near ruinous condition invited arson but inspired a successful effort to find a willing owner who rescued it. The garret of the wing has been stripped to its original "bones."

KITCHEN ADDITION

Stripped of the accretions of two and a half centuries, the wing is about to be restored. From left to right: plaster on stone wall; red paint on exterior door; panel door within red frame; whitewash on plaster wall; plaster on split and pit sawn lathe; a stairway to the cellar; and finally, a paneled wall and cupboards over the fireplace. To the experienced eye nearly all finished features, although mostly lost, are discernible from remnant details, what one might call the forensic pathology of old houses.

The Arriantje and Samuel Coeymans House

Coeymans, Albany County, New York

Blessed by Dutch inheritance rules Arriantje Coeymans (1672–c.1737), with her brother Samuel, jointly inherited much land and built the largest Dutch house ever in the Hudson River Valley. The explanation for such an unusually large house may come from the unique circumstances of its owners. Besides being heirs to considerable land and mill holdings, the unmarried siblings built the house for their mutual use and, no doubt seeking personal privacy, required separate bedrooms, necessitating the use of a second floor to accommodate them. Within five years Arriantje unexpectedly married David, of the prominent Ver Planck family, who was twenty-three years her junior. In commemoration, she had her portrait painted full length and life size.

The Coeymans house is the last of the grand early Dutch houses to survive—it was grand in size and conception. While outwardly Dutch (it originally had brick parapet gables, casement windows, and even a gable dormer with hoist entrance into the garret), inwardly its arrangement presaged a new manner of living: separate spaces for dining, sleeping, and socializing which were all accessed by common centralized hallways on two floors. That arrangement was fully realized in the 1790s when the house was extensively altered to the Georgian style, utilizing English jambed fireplaces, paneled walls with cupboards, and a lower gambrel roof.

FRONT EXTERIOR

Within the cramped confines of fortified towns in the old and new Netherlands, houses were customarily built upward to gain more room, often several stories high. In the countryside Dutch houses were more easily expanded laterally. The Coeymans house was a remarkable exception—it was built unusually large and on four levels. We can envision how and why this was done. The first level was the walk-in cellar with kitchen and, likely, some quarters for slaves and servants. The second level has its own ground-level entrance into a center hall with two large public rooms. The third level has the same configuration but these were undoubtedly the private rooms for the brother and sister. The garret was originally built for a front gable entry with hoist to accommodate the produce of the mills and farm.

SOUTH GABLE EXTERIOR

When the Coeymans house was modernized in 1795, its gable end was much altered. The high parapet gable roof was removed and a lower gambrel-roof framing installed, the gable brickwork relayed in American bond. Sash windows were for the first time installed in the gable end of the main floors, and larger ones put back in the garret. Many changes throughout the house were designed to modernize it in the Georgian style, ironically just as this pre-Revolution style was going out of fashion. This was about the last gambrel roof installed in the upper Hudson River Valley.

I also see [that you] are busy building, which was necessary, [though not] too heavy, as I understand that you have used such extra heavy beams for it, which only adds to the expense. If the house has a good foundation, the size of the beams does not matter so much, as long as they are strong enough to support the floor. But everyone follows his own taste in such matters.
—Jeremias van Rensselaer, Albany, 1659 [*Correspondence*, p. 199]

FRONT EXTERIOR

Nestled under the light shade of the small-leafed black locust tree, the Coeymans house appears to be an entirely Georgian house, yet the ghost of its original incarnation can be read from surviving details and a now lost 1730s painting. A resulting reconstruction (on paper) of the original house (*left*) displays all of its original medieval Dutch character: high pitch roof with parapet gables (including a rare central gable), two and four-light casement windows with alternating leaded casement and solid shutters, and atop the central garret gable once turned this lively stag weathervane. Such weather-forecaster ornaments, usually of animals, once topped many Dutch houses and some barns in the colonial period.

KITCHEN (CELLAR)

The cellar kitchen in the Coeymans house is as expansive and well finished as any first-floor room in other Dutch houses. The advantage of a kitchen in the cellar was the economical use of an existing space (instead of building a kitchen addition) and access to food kept in the cool storage of cellar rooms. Its disadvantage was the constant need to ascend stairs to the dining area and, as one colonialist observed, the difficulty of keeping an eye on what was going on among the servants and slaves that a first-floor, or separate, kitchen addition permitted.

Building against a hill such that the down-hill side of the cellar had level exit to the outside (as did the first floor on the uphill side) was an innovation for the Dutch not seen in the flatlands of The Netherlands (and thus less frequently found in the flatlands of Long Island and New Jersey).

The negroes in the North American colonies are treated more mildly and fed better than those in the West Indies. They have as good food as the rest of the servants, and they possess equal advantages in all things, except their being obliged to serve their whole lifetime and get no other wages than what their master's goodness allows them . . . no threats make more impression upon a negro here than that of sending him over to the West Indies, in case he will not reform.
—Peter Kalm, 1749–50 [*Travels*, p. 208]

DINING ROOM

When the house was "modernized" in the 1790s, albeit in a then old-fashioned Anglo-Dutch style, the Dutch fireplaces on three levels were replaced with English jambed fireplaces and, as here in the dining room, a paneled wall was erected, creating closets. It was in the far closet that an original casement window was left unchanged. Because the house was built with three levels of Dutch fireplaces it required a complex system of flues (one behind the other) with hearths and chimney all suspended from the beam structure; this is why the beams are so large.

BED BOX

Cupboard beds were common in The Netherlands and occasionally remarked on in early New York, but none survive intact in the New World. As a token to the mythology that enlivens our interest in the Dutch, this reproduction of a Dutch cupboard bed will serve well a new generation of children who will be read bedtime stories in their cozy nook. Here on the second floor we find a hall and two rooms, each once with an open Dutch fireplace framed with massive beams before the 1790s alterations to the Georgian style.

STAIRWAY

Dutch is bold. Their buildings and furnishings were bold in structure, elements, and colors. Seemingly they overbuilt for the ages. This staircase is twice the mass of its English equivalent. The stair balusters closely mimic in architecture those on tables made for the Dutch in New York and New Jersey. The use of gum-wood, a tree that grows primarily in New Jersey, for this stairway shows that the Coeymans were willing to pay a lot to create the right effect—a highly polished, richly colored surface.

CASEMENT WINDOW

When the Coeymans house was modernized in the Georgian mode in the 1790s, one early Dutch window with original painted shutters and leaded casements (now restored) survived because it was hidden from view by an enclosed passageway to the old house. Although dulled by the passage of time, the white, yellow, green, and orange of the frame and shutters testify to the vibrant sense of color the Dutch had.

The Teunise Slingerland House

Feura Bush, Albany County, New York

High up in the gable is a square tile incised "1762/ June/ TSL" to mark the completion date of the house by Teunise Slingerland. He is believed to be the grandson of the man of the same name who was the original settler in Feura Bush in the 1680s. Like so many other Dutch farmhouses, the house is located on a rise above a creek overlooking the alluvial fields which once constituted "Indian fields," a name once applied to a nearby site. The house is remarkable for its preservation of many original features and for its urban-Dutch configuration, that is, the brick gable end has an entrance door (the original and later high stoop having weathered away).

Built as a two-room-deep house with brick gables and stone sides, and a high basement, this house is similar to urban-style Dutch houses constructed in Albany up to this period. A frame addition to the two-room house was constructed in around 1840. At this time the brick parapet gable was reduced in height and covered with the deep molded fascia board visible here. Under its edge can be seen the evidence for the "tumbled" brickwork of the parapet and, at the peak, the bottom of what was a brick finial.

CELLAR DOOR

The cellar doorway of the Slingerland house is a rarity for it survives in its original red paint, the most commonly used color in early Dutch houses. With time and neglect the color has oxidized to a red brown, but where worn (*left*) some of its original intensity remains. An original exterior door to the back room of the house was recently discovered, covered by the addition in 1840, and retains its original bright red paint color, evidence of the original trim color on the exterior.

ENCLOSED STAIRWAY

Within just a few years of its erection the house was modernized with English fireplaces; the stairway was as well, its steep steps enclosed in paneled sheathing and with a door added. Undoubtedly the original stairway was enclosed but it was probably simpler in design. Its steepness reflects Dutch economy of space; its enclosure, an economy of warmth. Both purposes became less important in later generations as houses were expanded and upstairs spaces were inhabited, resulting in almost all such stairways becoming open and more gradual.

FIREPLACE, CELLAR KITCHEN

The Slingerland house originally had three open Dutch fireplaces set on the interior partition: two were back-to-back on the main floor and one, the large kitchen fireplace, was in the front cellar room. Within a generation the fireplaces were reconstructed with jambs in the English manner. This conversion had the advantage of creating space for a cupboard, originally on each side, likely appreciated by the housewife in a home without closets or other built-in storage.

HEARTH PAVER

Personalized mementos of an early time are rarely found associated with their maker. Among the hearth tiles of the first-floor fireplace is this one inscribed "Cornelis slengerlant," likely a son of the owner, with an image of a whitetail deer buck, as well as the stamped initials of the owner, TSL (Teunise Slingerland). This tile and the one in the front gable—both inscribed when wet and unfired—proclaim the fact that the Slingerlands were involved with the making of the bricks and tiles on their property, confirmation of an oft-repeated tradition that bricks were "made on the property." A Hudson Valley long fowler, the traditional flintlock hunting gun of the Dutch, is branded with the same TSL and was undoubtedly from this house; it dates from the same period, c. 1760.

The Mabee Farm

Rotterdam Junction, Schenectady County, New York
Schenectady County Historical Society, Schenectady, New York

The Mabee Farm remained in the family until recently when it became a museum consisting of a stone two-room house (c. 1725 or earlier), an attached one-room inn (c. 1790, although also Dutch in structure), and an adjacent "slave house" (c. 1760). A Dutch barn has also recently been re-erected.

On a high bank overlooking the Mohawk River west of Schenectady, this unique grouping of little altered structures tells a story of one family's farming, trading, and hospitality over three centuries. The steep-roofed stone house was once just one room, later doubled in size. Still surviving are parts of a Dutch fireplace and a cupboard bed, the latter a unique survival. The "slave house" is unconventional in height with two habitation rooms above a cellar, a feature at least consistent with use by slaves. The "inn" is a one-room structure that once served as a wayside tavern.

Except for the position of the doors, the slave house and inn were similar in size and structure, both designed to be minimal habitation for non-family members, set apart but close to the family home. An enclosed porch, added later, attached the inn to the house. Positioned close to the river and to the westward road, the Mabee home was a natural stopping place for travelers and traders.

THE MABEE HOUSES, EAST FACADE

The steep gable roof of the house bespeaks its earlier period, more akin to seventeenth-century houses than later ones. Most early builders were economical in their use of stone for walls. Above the first floor, the garret was unheated and, therefore, gable ends were usually finished cheaply and lightly with boards or shingles rather than stone. After it had been expanded to two rooms, the public side of the Mabee house was finished in stone to the ridge. This was done for looks rather than function, perhaps when the inn was built.

The extreme steepness of the roof is a New World holdover from Netherlandish construction designed for tile or thatch roofing materials. That steep pitch also assists sheathing boards to better overlap each other with beveled edges (a feature particularly of the upper Hudson River Valley), insuring extra weather tightness underneath a covering of wood shingles.

KITCHEN/SLAVE
AND MAIN HOUSE,
SOUTH FACADE,

*The Mabee Farm,
Rotterdam Junction,
NY.*

93

STAIRWAY

Looking from the newer east room towards the original room of the stone house, one sees an enclosed stairway. A mahogany armoire, circa 1830, serves the same storage purpose as the long gone *kas*. Through the paneled door, where a lamp now shines, was once a large Dutch fireplace, its original moldings and pilasters carefully stored away by the family for future discovery.

EAST ROOM

The east room of the stone house was added to the original one-room house by the mid-eighteenth century. It also once had a Dutch fireplace in the gable end where now an English-style fireplace exists. The position of an exterior door beside a fireplace is unusual, perhaps a later accommodation for access to the adjacent inn.

FIREPLACE, KITCHEN/
SLAVE HOUSE

The first-floor room of the kitchen/slave house once had a Dutch fireplace, bricked-in before the Revolution to form a chimney for a cellar fireplace. A mantle was affixed for show and a cupboard for use. This change moved the kitchen to the cellar leaving the main floor, and likely the garret as well, at least in warm weather, for habitation. These changes were consistent with accommodating slaves. An original enclosed stairway leads from cellar to garret room.

There may be no other Dutch structure that exists today that has remained essentially unchanged (even to the paint) since it was originally built. The eye today sees no less than what was seen over two centuries ago. The past is present in this house.

GARRET,
KITCHEN/SLAVE HOUSE

The garret is equally unchanged from the beginning, including the large hood chimney for the original Dutch fireplace. Unusually high walls gave ample headroom for work in the garret which was easily accessed by a stairway. The stairway was enclosed to trap heat on the first floor, suggesting that habitation, if not work, took place at the lower level.

96

The Rensselaer Nicoll House/Bethlehem House

Bethlehem Township, Albany County, New York

Bethlehem House is a residence rich in New York history and architectural distinction. Its builder was Rensselaer Nicoll (1707–1776). He and his wife Elizabeth Salisbury (b.1712) had English family names—they were descended from English officers who were among those to capture New York in 1664 and became prominent in its affairs, including marrying into leading Dutch families. Nicoll inherited from his mother's father Kiliaen Van Rensselaer (the Fourth Patroon—Second Lord—of Van Rensselaer Manor) thirteen hundred acres at Bethlehem just south of Albany in 1719. He was likely in residence by 1729 when he was a road commissioner there. The present house is believed to be dated 1735, the year of his marriage, although both might be earlier.

It is an imposing home, large and innovative for its time and place. It has thick load-bearing brick walls a full two-stories high with upstairs bedrooms and fireplaces. Young Nicoll's one concession to economy was to omit the center hall for a small front hall which functioned in the same way—separating the two main rooms from each other for privacy and both from the exterior doorway and outside temperature.

A large family cemetery south of the house commemorates its many inhabitants. Scattered among the family graves are small headstones bearing only the initials of the departed, family slaves. Caesar (1737–1852), a frequent name among slaves despite its exalted origins (it is the source for the titles Kaiser and Czar), was one who actually achieved a wider immortality for his one hundred fifteen years of service to the Nicoll family; this was commemorated more fittingly by a large stone long after his death.

SOUTH GABLE FACADE

Bethlehem House was constructed on a four-room plan; it is two-stories high with a gambrel roof. Its structure and decoration are primarily English and predate the general acceptance of this type of house in the upper Hudson River Valley by a generation. A notable earlier exception was Elizabeth Salisbury Nicoll's family home near Catskill which likely influenced her new home's design. From its 1705 beginning, the house of her father Francis Salisbury was the most progressive in the upriver region, having a gambrel roof, center hall, and rooms on two floors. The south facade of the Nicoll house portrays the original height and roof line of the 1735 house, but one room was extended on this end in 1795. Until recent times the upper part of the gambrel roof was enclosed in a decorative balustrade. The low wing, circa 1810–12, comprises a double kitchen.

HALL ENTRY AND DINING ROOM

In some fine Anglo-Dutch houses, floors painted like marbled tiles were known, inspiring this recent treatment. A connecting door joins the two main rooms of Rensselaer Nicoll's stylish home. The foreground was once a small entry hall for the front door, leading to a parlor and seen here, a dining room.

Portraits of Dutch King William and his English wife, Queen Mary, symbolize the royal union of joint monarchs at a time when New Yorkers were blending Dutch and English culture within their homes.

DINING ROOM

Long ago a concession to new fashion prompted the removal of the original panel wall and cupboards to a less public room. In its place are paintings equally suited to this home. At either side are portraits of Abraham Lott and his wife Geertruy (Gertrude) Coeymans. He had been here before (in the flesh, as likely had his wife, whose family home was nearby). In his 1774 journal he wrote of visiting the Nicolls at Bethlehem House.

Early home furnishings have always reflected the allegiances, faith, and worldly interests of their owners. The scripture painting over the mantle is New York Dutch, as much an emblem of identity and faith. It depicts the finding of Moses, a prophet who led the enslaved Israelites out of subjugation, a theme the Dutch easily identified with as they were also a small nation beset by powerful enemies.

Although lost from use, but not from documentation, a crumb cloth covers the floor, a reminder of the neat and clean virtues of early (and latter day) housewives.

HALL TO DINING ROOM.

With a leg in each culture, the furnishings shown here derive from Dutch and English sources. The chairs are from London and Boston, and the portraits are from England. The *kas* or cupboard is a Dutch form made in New York. The purpose of the *kas* was to store and secure valuables such as textiles (clothes, bedding, curtains), in addition to silver and other valuables. In America the *kas* was built of local hardwoods such as gumwood, maple, and sycamore, which have a desirable wavy grain.

One room . . . in the greater house [Schuyler Flatts] was opened for the reception of company; all the rest were bedchambers for their accommodation, while the domestic friends of the family occupied neat little bed-rooms in the attics, or in the winter house . . . the winter rooms had carpets; the lobby had oil-cloth painted in lozenges, to imitate blue and white marble. The best bedroom was hung with family portraits, some of which were admirably executed; and in the eating room, which, by the bye, was rarely used for that purpose, were some fine scripture paintings. —Anne Grant, Albany, 1756–63 [*Memoirs*, p. 170]

NORTH BEDROOM

The north bedroom of Bethlehem retains its original English fireplace and Georgian paneled wall, innovations in the Albany area which took a generation for others to emulate. Not dependent on a heavy wood structure to support Dutch fireplaces, as in the Coeymans house (see p. 79), this house could be built of lighter timbers and thinner masonry walls. The English house provided a newer style, with more of a variety of spaces, and a greater efficiency of operation. It also was less expensive to build—a savings that was often put back into more expensive decoration.

The Palatine Lutheran Church

Mohawk Valley, Route 5, Montgomery County, New York
The Palatine Society of the Evangelical Lutheran Church, Inc.,
Nelliston, New York

The Palatine Germans and Netherlands Dutch were nearly contiguous in geography and culture both in the fatherlands and in the New World. Many Germans came to New York, first settling as a unit at Germantown in what is now Columbia County in 1710. From there they spread north westward into the Mohawk and Schoharie River Valleys, which were newly opened Mohawk Indian lands. Their early houses are indistinguishable from those built by the Dutch (while Germans in Pennsylvania did adopt Palatine features to local materials), including their churches. Both groups lived adjacent to each other in small communities—their harmony derived from a similar culture, language, and faith. They also shared a more difficult fate in the Mohawk River Valley: the exposed military frontier during the French and Indian War and the Revolution suffered though a multitude of fires set to homes and to barns as Tory and allied Iroquois periodically swept through the valley. What did happen to survive the general destruction were churches, such as this 1770 limestone structure.

INTERIOR
OF THE CHURCH PULPIT

In recent years the church's interior has been largely restored to its earlier appearance, including straight-back pews arranged to face from three directions, with the raised pulpit set on the center of a long wall opposite the front door. The restored pulpit is shaped like a goblet with a sounding board above which, according to an early pastor, was "intended to arrest the preacher's words in their upward flight, and fling them back upon the ears of the worshipers."

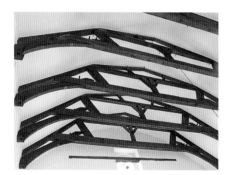

ROOF TRUSS

The gambrel roof truss of the Palatine Church is more complex than any other seen to date, consisting of double collar beams and multiple braces. This is the result of wishing to build without intruding anchor beams (to tie the walls together), thus the truss must serve this purpose as well stablizing a tall structure against wind pressure and spanning an unusually wide space (thirty-six feet).

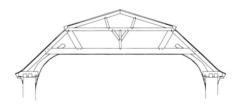

DRAWING OF ROOF TRUSS

The complex gambrel roof truss was designed to handle stresses from multiple directions: the weight of a heavy and wide roof, the lateral wracking from wind pressure, and remain rigidly stiff while tying the stone walls together.

EXTERIOR

The Palatine Stone Church, as this Lutheran church has long been known, was erected in 1770 to serve the mostly German settlement around Palatine on the north bank of the Mohawk River. Its steeple was changed and further alterations ensued in the early nineteenth century, but the chance visitor would be quite taken aback by the early feeling one gets in this out-of-the-way sanctuary.

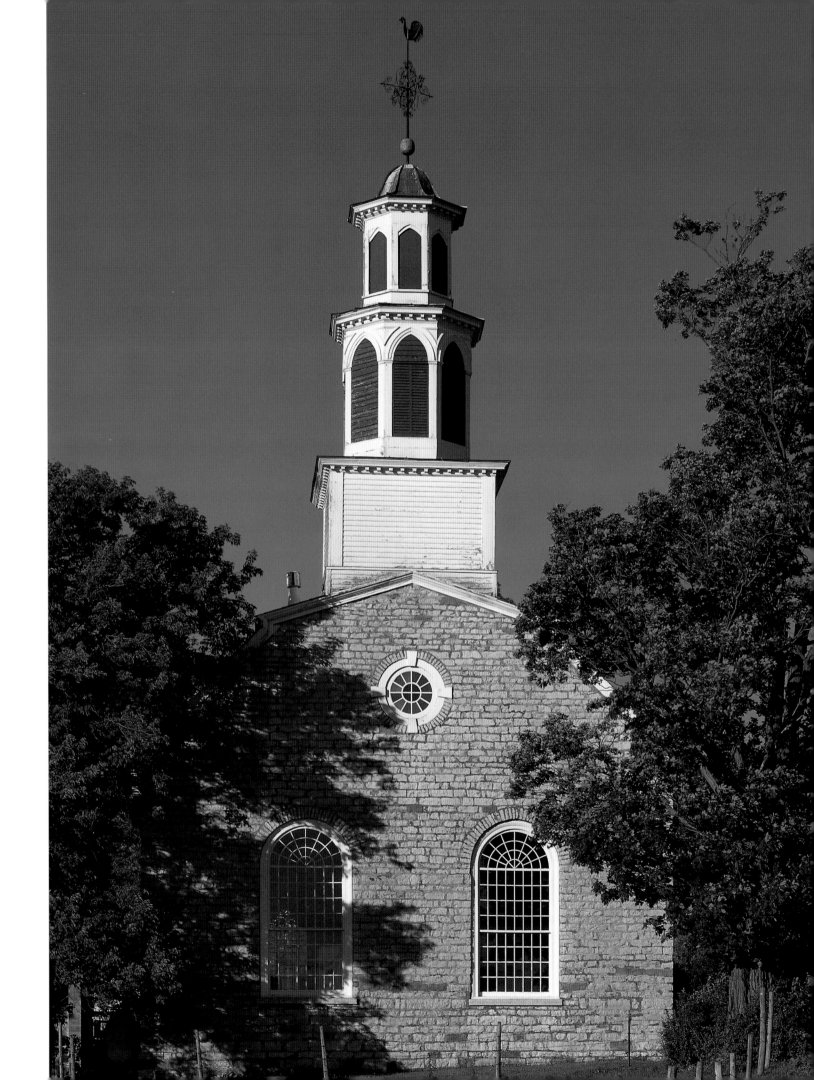

Dutch Barns
In the Mohawk and Upper Hudson River Valleys

Until a century ago ninety percent of Americans lived on farms, the architectural essence of which was, and still is, the barn. Immigrants from England, Germany, Sweden, and The Netherlands adapted their Old World barn types to New World frontier life and materials. Every Dutch farm had a variety of farm structures usually including a hay barrack (sometimes two or more), sheep fold, pig sty, chicken house, corn crib, work shed, and occasionally, more specialized structures. But on every farm was a house and a barn. The barn served multiple purposes, including sheltering a few work horses and milk cows for domestic use. However, it was primarily there to store hay and grain. Most Dutch farms were based on cash crops, producing and selling various grains, especially wheat, as well as peas and corn. The Dutch barn was well suited to processing and storing grain as a description of its structure reveals.

The Dutch barn has an ancient lineage dating back at least a millennium. Its basic structure was little changed over this period and for the centuries it was built in the New World. From the outside one sees a nearly square structure (most are forty- to fifty-feet wide and deep (D17) with a high pitch roof extending to relatively low side walls, the entry doors being in the gable ends (D16). A wagon of hay or grain sheaves entered one of these central doors into a wide central aisle. The aisle is framed by a series of H-bents, as in a Dutch house, except that the posts are larger and extended higher. On long plates, support rafters which extend from the apex of the roof outward beyond the posts and plates to an outer wall create a side aisle on both sides of the central aisle. Dutch barns are thus three-aisle barns. Most who enter them are struck by their immense space and resemblance to Gothic cathedrals. In fact the resemblance is historical, for both derive from the same medieval principles of construction—H-bent framing defining a nave and side aisles.

The Dutch farmer then pitched his crop up onto a flooring of sapling poles laid from one anchor beam to the next. The wagon was then driven out through the other gable door to the gaze of horses and cows stabled in the side aisles. When dried, wheat sheaves were thrown down to the barn floor where they were crushed (by flails or an ingenious horse-drawn rotating cone) and grain separated from the chaff by winnowing in the wind. Grain was bagged and sent to the gristmill to be ground into flour and shipped to the nearest city.

Today only six hundred Dutch barns survive in various states, far fewer than their companion Dutch houses. No longer adaptable to contemporary dairy farming, they are neglected and are disappearing at a fast rate. Some have been reprieved as barn museums, homes, offices, workshops, and garages.

Greater Wemp Barn

Feura Bush, Albany County, New York

This large Dutch barn once stood on the south bank of the Mohawk River in upstate New York, not far from Fort Hunter adjacent to a smaller Dutch barn—the Lesser Wemp Barn. Today it stands restored on a farm in Feura Bush, New York, secure and tight for another two hundred years. It has been given a second life, perhaps in gratitude for its role in bringing modern atten-

tion to the preservation of this most distinct of colonial farm structures. In 1962 it was the first Dutch barn seen by John Fitchen, a professor of architecture, who was so impressed with the quality of its construction that he devoted years to the study of the New World Dutch barn and published the definitive book by that title. The book has spawned a movement to save the hundreds of Dutch barns that survive, many just barely, throughout the Dutch settlement areas.

The Barn at the Mabee Farm

Rotterdam Junction, Schenectady County, New York
Schenectady County Historical Society, Schenectady, New York

This large Dutch barn (The Nilsen barn, after recent owners, the original owner is not known) was recently removed from a site near Johnstown, New York, in the Mohawk River Valley, that was designated for development. Its massiveness suggests an early structure, perhaps pre-Revolutionary. If so, a rare survival from a time when almost all barns on this military frontier were burned down during enemy raids. Its massive anchor beams (thirty-five feet long, twenty-two feet deep) attest to the virgin forests of the Mohawk River Valley which beckoned settlers, encouraged by generous terms provided by William Johnson (1715–1774), the owner of most of the land in this part of the valley.

SCRIBE MARKS

Carpenters' scribe marks, here a vertical line with two semi-circles, vary with each builder's preference, but its purpose is the same—to set a reference mark before cutting mortise and tenon. It marks two feet from the back of the column through which this large anchor beam is to be tenoned.

ANCHOR BEAM JOINT

In the process of being reconstructed, each **H** bent of the barn has been braced by a board and a wedge through the exposed tenon. Next, the other wedge and three trunnels ("tree nails" or oak pins) will be driven into place. When the long plate has been lifted and set upon the top of the posts with its own braces to the post, the **H**-frame will be self-supporting.

FRAME (DUTCH BARN)

During construction (or reconstruction in this case) a barn is the main star of a community ballet, each "dancer" balancing self and timbers until the climax when all timbers are joined in a perfect whole—a balance of dynamic stress and tension now transformed into an immutable work of art for the ages. What is accomplished here in hours once took centuries to complete: the Gothic stone cathedral is the collateral ancestor of the three-aisle Dutch barn.

The Dunckel Barn
Mohawk River Valley, Nelliston, NY

Peter Dunckel (1750-1830) was a Palatine German who emigrated to America in 1766, establishing a farm in the Mohawk River Valley and served in the militia during the Revolution, including the nearby Battle of Oriskany. He built this large Dutch-style barn about 1780-90. As originally built (and moved and rebuilt as such) it was fifty feet wide across the gable entrance and forty-five feet deep. It differs from other Dutch barns in the unusual height of its side walls (nineteen feet) and total height to the peak (forty-three feet), both measures conducive to storing extra amounts of grain. While the main anchor beams are of white pine (twelve by twenty-four inches in section), all the outer framing is of elm. This species is most unusual in early barns, although the fact that "Rock elm" was once prevalent in this part of the Mohawk Valley may account for its use, having a reputation for becoming "rock" hard with age. Before being clad in weatherboards and shingles, a Dutch barn's dramatic structure is revealed, especially against the black of night.

Wemple Barn

Rotterdam Junction, Schenectady County, New York

Long unused but not abused, the Wemple barn shows
how well old barns can survive even if only the minimum
of effort is taken to protect the roof and siding from the
weather. Even the white pine siding, which is two centuries
old and warped, split, and re-nailed, survives and performs
its function.

The barn, built by a Van Wemp (later Wemple, as they were
Tories who changed their name after the Revolution) may
date from as early as the 1730s but the property was later
owned by Jacob Delamont who built an adjacent brick
gambrel-roof house about 1760, a likely latest date for the
barn. The regularity of the barn's proportions and the even
hewing of timbers is unusual, indicating craftsmanship by a
master builder. These qualities plus its state of preservation
make this one of the finest extant Dutch barns in America.

AISLE DOOR

Like so many features of Dutch houses
and barns, the Dutch "nail pad" hinge has
a purpose beyond its appealing from. Its
nails penetrate the vertical siding and a
horizontal batten (plank) on the inside of
the door. If all nails were in a line they
might split the batten along its grain and
weaken the door, but with two nails offset
the door is secure, even with a split.

GABLE

Remarkably the Wemple barn retains its original doors and gable siding—including the ventilation holes in the upper gable know as "martin holes" after Purple Martins, birds appreciated by Dutch farmers for their penchant for driving off hawks and crows. The wagon doors are mounted on wooden pins and hinges and are unusual in that they swing inward. The side aisle doors swing outward on long iron hinges. This barn is notable for its height (thirty-six feet), steep roof, and relatively low sides.

INTERIOR

The frame of this forty-seven-foot-wide by fifty-six-foot-long barn is massive but finely constructed of pitch pine, the preferred and predominant wood used by the Dutch for construction in the upper Hudson River Valley. Hard and heavy, it made strong building timbers which were resistant to moisture and vermin. The steep pitch of the roof and the long sway braces (extending from the purlin plate to the columns at a point below the massive anchor beams) are indicators of a pre-Revolution barn.

Therein [the barn] we lodge all our grain' and within, many operations are performed, such as threshing, and cleaning of flax and husking the corn, etc. Therein the horses are stabled and the oxen stall-fed. In the summer, the women resort to it in order to spin their wool. The neatness of our boarded floors, the great draught of air caused by the open doors, which are always made wide enough to permit a loaded wagon to enter, and their breadth afford [the women] an opportunity of spinning long threads, of carding at their ease. . . . All classes of our cattle, our sheep, our calves must be placed by themselves, ands have in each division convenient racks and bars in order to communicate easily from one to another. —J. Hector St. John de Crevecoeur, Orange County, NY, 1782, [*Sketches*, pp. 312–3]

The Peter Gremps Dutch Barn
(*also known as* **Fredericks Barn**)
Stone Arabia, Montgomery County, New York

On the high ground north of the Mohawk River and near the village of Palatine Bridge is a place called Stone Arabia, not alluding to the Empty Quarter of Arabia but, it is claimed, to "stone turnips" (German: *steen rabi*). Some believe it is a reference to stones which are heaved up by frost each spring and must be cleared from the fields. The near absence of stone walls in the area makes this conjecture doubtful, but colorful explanations are the enduring backbone of folk tales. More likely it is a comment on the quality of locally grown turnips.

In recent years this barn has been known as Fredericks Barn, after the family that continues to farm this land. In earlier times it was owned by the Gremps, possible descendants of Crems or Krems who may have been part of the German migration into this area in 1724. Peter Gremps was in possession of the farm at the time this barn was probably built, post-Revolution.

BARN

In a century in which more trees have grown in upstate New York than at any time since the Revolution, it is unusual to see a barn sitting off by itself in a field. But that was normal through much of the nineteenth century as the wooded frontier was cleared by a rapidly expanding agrarian nation, each farm carefully fostering a wood lot, their only source of heating fuel. Progress had drawbacks as exposed barns received the full force of storm winds and lightning.

SIDING (EXTERIOR)

In the colonial period and long after, barn siding was not painted—the natural ability of pine to shed water and dry off was all that was needed to keep the barn tight and dry. Some Dutch barns survive today with original unpainted siding, now two centuries old. If kept nailed tight they can survive for many more years. Painting barns was a nineteenth-century decorative idea, continued to this day for that reason but also because of the mistaken assumption that it is functionally necessary.

Dutch barns were built without side windows. This one may be an early exception in order to light the granary bins within; their security from theft insured by wrought iron bars.

GABLE (EXTERIOR)

Barn framing provides a lesson in the artful application of opposing forces. The roof and siding boards protect the frame and the barn's contents from wind, temperature extremes, and precipitation. The tightness that gives protection, however, increases the weight of snow and the pressure of wind on the frame, requiring heavy columns and purlin plates, wall posts and plates, and rafters to counteract this weight, and lateral and longitudinal braces and struts to resist the wind. The large anchor beams are just that, the anchor which holds all the other timbers in place.

GRANARY

Rare among surviving barns is this granary, a storeroom for grain. Early accounts speak of storing grain in the garret of the house and in the barn, although one farmer lamented the losses to rats in the latter case.

WOODEN HINGE

The large wagon doors of Dutch barns are secured with wrought iron hinges or, as with this barn, wooden hinges, here set upon a wood pintle secured to the door post by iron spikes and an iron staple.

Kilts Barn

Stone Arabia, Montgomery County, New York

Peter Kilts purchased land from Philip Livingston in 1752 within the Stone Arabia Patent. On this he established a farm which remained in the family until 1972. Like most barns in this region, it likely dates from just after the Revolution.

EXTERIOR

Part of the fascination of structures, especially those imbued with the aura of age, is how they present themselves so differently as their appearance is altered by weather, seasons, and time. Like a runway model whose dress, hair, makeup, and gait transforms her into another being, barns exude quite different personalities with these changes. Alone on a grassy field under a pure blue sky, bright sun brings out sharply contrasting planes and colors transforming for the moment this barn into a work of art.

The Hudson Highlands

Ulster, Dutchess, Westchester, Orange, and Rockland Counties

The Hudson River is navigable for one hundred fifty miles, from New York City north to Albany. But no early settlement took place in this region because there was widespread fear of the Native Americans as a consequence of wars against them prosecuted by Kieft, the governor in the 1640s. Settlement was also hindered by topography. The entire region on the west side of the river is dominated by stratified limestone hills and the Catskill Mountains which almost block off the interior valleys from access to the Hudson River.

Ulster County

Not until 1653 were some disgruntled Dutchmen at Rensselaerswyck enticed by freehold land to come to what is now Ulster County. At first they built rudimentary houses overlooking fertile flats along the Esopus Creek. Prudently they clustered them behind a palisaded enclosure for defense, calling their village Wiltwyck (now Kingston). Although they built their initial houses hastily, using wood, they began building one- and two-room stone houses within a decade, making use of the limestone that was otherwise a hindrance to transport and farming. The Dutch continued to construct this same type of stone house for nearly two centuries, preferring this material almost to the exclusion of any other. The persistence of this house type, unchanged for so long, is remarkable. It may partially be explained by the isolation these farms experienced, being separated from each other by substantial streams and long parallel ranges of hills. What drew the Dutch to the interior was the extensive alluvial flat lands along the Wallkill River, Rondout Creek, and their tributaries. These valleys extended to the south and southwest, forming corridors of communication all the way to western New Jersey, which drew Dutch settlers to that otherwise isolated region in the late seventeenth century.

The availability of freehold land in these valleys in what became Ulster County encouraged large numbers of settlers throughout the last half of the seventeenth century. This influx, however, diminished in the next century as the valleys filled up, even leading to a net outflow of offspring of original settlers. The result: many farms remained in families even into the twentieth century. This further preserved traditional patterns of life. Not surprisingly, a remarkable number of houses have survived with little structural alteration. Just in the township of Marbletown in the Rondout Valley, over one hundred and thirty stone houses are extant. In this and adjacent townships there may be more stone houses than any comparable area among the original thirteen colonies.

The Dutch were not the only settlers in this region. A group of Huguenots, French Protestants, acquired a patent to land on the Wallkill River south of Wiltwyck in 1677. They formed a compact community still called New Paltz which retains on its "Stone House Street" much of its original appearance. Here you can still visit homes of the Hasbrouck, Du Bois, and Deyo families which are the same in structure as Dutch stone houses elsewhere, the one exception is that they are built together as a village, a rare feature in the Hudson Valley where farmsteads were almost always disbursed on their own land. In this respect New Paltz and Kingston were more like New England communities where defensive clustering was prevalent because of the fear of Native Americans. There were attacks in the 1640s, as well as at Wiltwyck between 1659–63. Nearby New Dorp (Hurley) was burned in 1663. During the Revolution, over a century later, Indian and Tory raids took place in the Rondout Valley and Kingston was burned by British troops. Because of such stirring events and the persistence of original families even into the twentieth century, Ulster County continues to have a strong sense of history that surpasses that of other counties.

While Scots and Irish did migrate into southern parts of the county (and gave Ulster its name), it has not otherwise been inundated by urban and suburban sprawl as most other Hudson River Valley counties have in our lifetime, leaving much of its valley landscapes dotted with open farmland and stone houses as if the past was still present.

Dutchess County

Across the Hudson River from Ulster is the equally large county of Dutchess. Settlement in this, and other adjacent counties,

Jean Hasbrouck House
New Paltz, Ulster County, New York

Previous page: This original chimney is stagger-
ing in size, three feet by nine feet at the base
and twenty-six-feet high to the roof line. Even
more remarkable, it and the Dutch fireplace
below (p. 128-129) have both survived intact
when all others have been altered or removed
from the colonial houses of New York and
New Jersey. This house retains many other
original or early features which merit its special
distinction as one of the most important of
colonial structures.

was influenced by the prevailing topography and Indian
relations, but was altered by the original land-holding scheme.
The east side of the river does not have the rugged terrain of its
westward counterpart, nor exposure to the frontier, and thus
has less stone suitable for building and less contact with Indians.
In addition Dutchess County was not taken up by patroonships
and manors as some other counties were. It was composed of
speculative land grants issued to a few individuals or partners
by the governor and confirmed by the British government as
Crown patents. Ten patents were issued between 1685 and
1706, all purchased amicably from the Indians before each
patent was issued, a precedent which alleviated the hostilities
experienced in Ulster County. While some patentees may have
wished to set themselves up like manors for the purpose of leas-
ing land to tenants, it was soon obvious that selling land would
bring in far more settlers. As a result, independent freeholding
became the settlement pattern of this county.

Among the first patentees was Pieter Schuyler. As a member
of the governor's council, sometimes lieutenant-governor,
and governor-appointed mayor of Albany he was the arche-
type of the evolving Anglo-Dutch patrician group that par-
layed political finesse and entrepreneurial savvy into powerful positions and wealth. One of the obvious ways this
group could increase its assets was in land speculation,
receiving large tracts of land from the governor
("The Crown") at small consideration as a quid-pro-quo
for political allegiance.

Within a half dozen years the patentees began selling off
farm plots to other Dutchmen along the fertile stream-side
lands near the Hudson River, specifically at Poughkeepsie,
at the valley of the Vis Kill, and at Kipsburgen (later
Rhinebeck). By the 1730s a mix of Dutch, Huguenot,
Walloon, and German families had settled there. But in
the ensuing two decades, Dutchess County was discovered
by large numbers of New Englanders who acquired lands in
the eastern half of the county. At the same time many families of mostly Dutch descent came to the western valleys
from Long Island, New Jersey, and nearby Westchester
County.

In Dutchess County houses were as varied as their origins.
Settlers from New England mostly built wood houses as
they had always done. In the western or Dutch portion most
houses were of stone, much like those in other upriver counties: a story-and-a-half high with a pitch roof, one and two
rooms, and quite plain. There are now, and were once, more
clapboard and shingle-sheathed houses in the Dutch region
of this county, possibly the influence of migrants from the
lower countries and New Jersey, although their form and
plan match the local stone equivalents.

Stone houses built by Germans, who came with the great
migration of three thousand Palatines to Livingston Manor
in Albany (now Columbia) County in 1710, are essentially the
same as those built by the Dutch. Indeed, despite long speculation on how houses built for or by Germans were distinctive,
no attribute has been found to be so prevalent amongst them
that it can be said that they are distinctively Germanic. Cellar
kitchens, sometimes said to be a German feature, are found in
many German-owned houses, yet they also occur in Dutch-
built houses, especially those on hillier ground where ground-
level entrances to cellars as well as the first floor are possible.

There are just a few brick houses in this county, mostly built
between 1750–70 and with gambrel roofs. As such they
closely relate to the same Anglo-Dutch–style houses of this
form built in Albany county at the same time, primarily
English in form and function, with elements of Dutch structure in their framing and details.

The advantages of Dutchess County, which resulted in its
quick expansion during the mid-eighteenth century, were
relatively fertile lands close to the Hudson River—convenient to transportation to New York City—and a freehold
land system which attracted the most ambitious farmers.
Those attributes carried the county's prosperity well into the
nineteenth century.

Westchester County

South of Dutchess County is Westchester County (skip-
ping over small and hilly Putnam County, which was split

off from Westchester) which extends right down to the island of Manhattan. Being close to New York City it was attractive to the wealthy Anglo-Dutch, primarily the Van Cortlandt (1697) and Philipse (1693) families. They established manors along the Hudson River while others created four smaller manors adjacent to New York City and the Long Island Sound. Except for Van Cortlandt's manor, which extended to the Connecticut boundary, much of the eastern part of the county was open to New Englanders who quickly settled there. Dutch settlement, as in Dutchess County, was near the Hudson River and on the manors, all leasehold. The manors, understandably, did not attract the number of settlers they desired and often those who did come did not stay. By the second quarter of the eighteenth century ambitious sons moved off to neighboring counties (Dutchess and Orange) where they could acquire their own farms. As a result, relatively few houses were built and far fewer survive today. The homes were built of the conventional stone-house type similar to those in other river counties. Of the later Anglo-Dutch brick houses similar to those in northern counties, only a small number were said to have been built and none exist today. What does remain are the manor owners' houses: Van Cortlandt Manor House at Croton and Philipsburg, the residence-cum-warehouse on Philipse Manor at Tarrytown.

Orange County

Orange County is on the west side of the river across from Westchester and just south of Ulster. It was also freehold land, divided up in a series of small patents and sold off to settlers, this time primarily Scots and Irish. After 1717 Jacobites from the Highlands, including many refugees from the 1715 and 1745 rebellions, and Scots-Irish Presbyterians from Irish Ulster began to make up a new wave of immigrants to New York. They spread into Orange County and then up into the southern part of Ulster County. At the same time Dutch families were resettling out of the manors of Westchester into freehold land in Orange and elsewhere. Their stone residences are still found along the river-bordering lands of Orange County.

Rockland County

Culture areas respect no modern boundaries and Rockland County, while in New York, is culturally a part of Bergen County just across the border in New Jersey. Isolated by mountains from Orange County in New York, of which it was long a part, Rockland County was settled by the Dutch of Bergen County. The first land division was a large patent acquired in 1681 by a group of Dutchmen from Manhattan and New Jersey who purchased the land for their own use, not for speculation. Other patents followed both to Dutch and English purchasers but settlement was primarily in the southeast part of the county close to the Hudson River and away from the high hills in the west.

In most respects the houses here are similar to those in Bergen County—a pitch roof if one-room deep, a gambrel roof if more than one-room deep, and with or without center halls. The overhanging eave is prevalent. Like Bergen County, almost exclusive use was made of the abundant supply of red sandstone. In Rockland County there is, and was, a greater proportion of the smaller, one-room-deep houses, which is to be expected in areas that had not the time to develop the prosperity associated with larger houses.

The Jean Hasbrouck House

New Paltz, Ulster County, New York
The Huguenot Historical Society, New Paltz, New York

Jean Hasbrouck, born near Calais, France in around 1643, was a Huguenot who fled religious persecution with other members of his family (Abraham, p. 130). He went to the German Palatinate in the 1660s where he married another Huguenot, Anna Deyo. Jean was one of twelve patentees of the New Paltz Patent on which these interrelated families settled by 1678, having lived briefly with the Dutch at nearby New Dorp (p. 145). At New Paltz they built rudimentary houses and cleared fields to farm. It was not until the 1690s, however, that they were able to build the stone houses we see today. Likely this one dates, at least in part, from about 1694, when his brother's nearby home was built.

Jean Hasbrouck's house is structurally unique for its place and period. It has a central hall with two large rooms on either side and interior partition fireplaces, an advanced plan accepted only decades later in the Hudson River Valley. Bridging this large house (forty-two feet by forty-nine feet) is a roof, conventional in its high pitch form with rafter and collar beam framing, but built as large as a barn roof. It is twice the size and height of any other roof in its region, posing a unique structural problem: how to insure its strength against wind pressure and snow load. This was resolved with unconventional bracing (p. 33).

FRONT OF HOUSE

Unlike other houses in the village, the unusually high gable walls of Jean Hasbrouck's house are of wood, not stone which was likely deemed too vulnerable to stand on its own without the corner tie-ins of the lower walls. A later pentice at the front door offers prudent protection from the quantities of rain that cascade off such a high roof.

KITCHEN

Of the four large rooms of this early
center-hall house, the room at the left
rear has remained unchanged; its original
Dutch fireplace (and hood chimney) is
still intact, the only one so preserved in
this condition. Slightly altered is the back
wall of the hearth which once had a flat
whitewashed surface, a fire back set at
floor level. An opening into a five-plate
stove iron in the next room provided
warmth there without an open fire.

The Abraham Hasbrouck House

New Paltz, Ulster County, New York
The Huguenot Historical Society, New Paltz, New York

Abraham Hasbrouck was born in Calais, France, in the
1650s, a younger brother of Jean, also an original patentee
of New Paltz. They married sisters, daughters of patentee
Christian Deyo. They all arrived at their new land in 1678,
building temporary wood homes while expanding cultivated
lands. In the 1690s they began to build stone houses.
Abraham's 1694 house consists of the middle one-room
section of the present three-room house. Like most such
small pioneer houses it was soon expanded so that when his
son Daniel inherited it in 1717 there were two more rooms,
one to the north, seen here, and one to the south. The
house remained in the family, with little changed, for
nearly two centuries.

One of the distinctive features of this house is its exposed
chimney. Exterior chimneys are associated with warm cli-
mates, such as in Virginia or the Carolinas, where heat dissi-
pation to the outside is more important than retention on
the inside. From Maryland northward into New England,
chimneys are usually on the inside—winter warmth is more
imperative than summer cooling. In New York and New
Jersey the issue of too much interior summer heat was
resolved by building "summer" kitchens. In this region the
exterior chimney does occur in houses with cellar fireplaces.
The chimney is stepped out to allow the flue of the first-
floor fireplace straight passage to the roof inside the gable
wall. The Hasbrouck house is a curious exception. Although
a step-out chimney was provided, no first-floor fireplace was
built, nor even framed for its future construction.

GABLE CHIMNEY

The north gable of Abraham Hasbrouck's
house gives evidence of the sole fireplace
in the cellar. While economically providing
heat to two rooms from the fireplace below,
the lack of adequate window light in the
cellar must have made the chore of cooking
that much more taxing.

BEDROOM

In the north section of Abraham Hasbrouck's home, the first-floor room displays furnishings associated with eighteenth-century New York. Evidence of early blue paint on the walls inspired this unusual color. In most houses multiple layers of whitewash testify to the dirt caused by the open Dutch fireplace. This room, however, was without a fireplace; its walls remained clean and its early color was evident. It received warmth from the kitchen below through a hole in the floor.

The Johannes Decker House
Wallkill, Ulster County, New York

For two centuries the Decker family resided on this farm and, if they were to return today, they would recognize it with ease for it is little changed. Cornelis Decker acquired a land patent here in 1694 and is said to have built a log home nearby on the Shawangunk Kill. His son Johannes inherited the farm and built a one-room stone house, the center of the present extended home, in 1720–26, the dates of his two marriages. In 1735 he added a room to the left side of the house (the "old kitchen," as it came to be known). His son Cornelis (1732–1812) was the youthful inheritor of the home in 1742. In the 1780s he added a hall and room to the right, and an extension to the center rear, reportedly to house his ten slaves, of whom he owned more than almost anyone in the district.

FRONT OF HOUSE

The house's expansions likely reflected the farm's prosperity—by the late eighteenth century it was founded more on wheat as a cash crop than merely a subsistence economy. Cornelis' eldest son Johannes (1767–1814) briefly inherited the home in 1812, but was succeeded by his brother John Dupuy Decker (1799–1881) who improved the house with a long piazza and further acreage. Not until 1910 did the farm pass out of the family. It is still a farm; the Indian maize fields of three centuries ago still come forth each year with this crop and the Dutch barn is filled with hay for horses. For a fortunate few the pastoral spirit is born again in every generation, assuring some farms continue as such.

. . . you will find his [a Dutchman's] house and farm to be the neatest in all the country; and you will judge by his wagon and fat horses that he thinks more of the affaires of this world than of those of the next. He is sober and laborious; therefore, he is all he ought to be as to the affaires of his life. As for those of the next, he must trust to the great Creator. Each of these people instruct their children as well as they can, but these instructions are feeble compared to those which are given to the youth of the poorest class in Europe. —J. Hector St. John de Crevecoeur: Orange County, New York, 1782 [*Sketches*, p. 75]

134

SOUTH GABLE

The west or "old kitchen" gable betrays its purpose by the extension of an oven out of the back wall of its fireplace. Sheathed against weather by a roof and wood siding, the oven was a common feature of Dutch houses, providing the means to turn grain into food. Some were separate beehive-shaped structures; others were like this one, incorporated into the back wall of Dutch fireplaces. Later English fireplaces incorporated them into one widened jamb.

The front porch or "piazza" of the Decker house was built in the early nineteenth century although its appearance and function relates closely to the earlier (though some later) extended eaves on Dutch houses south of this region, including a smoothed transition between the roof angles.

HALL

In 1787 Cornelis Decker expanded his house in an altogether typical manner for the Dutch: He added this hall and a room creating, in effect, a center-hall house with this passageway (Van Alen House p. 62). It provided the means to communicate to the outside along with protection from winter cold in adjacent rooms, and increased their privacy in a farm family with many slaves.

Many of the old Dutch farmers in this country, have . . . Slaves about their house. To their care and management every thing is left; the oldest farmer manages the lands, directs the cultivation of it and without consulting him the master can do nothing; he is in fact in general the more intelligent of the two; and so as the master can but exist in the enjoyment and contentment of ease, he is content to become the Slave of the Slave . . . —William Strickland, 1794–95 [*Journal*]

DINING ROOM

The original room that comprised Johannes Decker's first house of, circa 1720–26, has a late-eighteenth-century fireplace and cupboards. A transom molding over the door to the "old kitchen" is a decorative effect (for plate display) found in some earlier houses of this region. Around a seventeenth-century Netherlands table are a group of "York" chairs, typical of New York turners' work in the late eighteenth century.

NORTH ROOM

The most modern of the house's rooms is the 1787 east room. With an English-style fireplace, a wall of cupboards, and a ceiling once plastered, it was Decker's concession to fancy living and, as such, likely served as a parlor, appropriately distanced from the activities of the old rooms of the house.

139

"OLD KITCHEN"

During the expansion of the house in the 1780s, all Dutch fireplaces were upgraded to the English style. In other houses this meant creating bedrooms with fireplaces in the garret, but not here. To this day no fireplaces exist upstairs, indicating that the Dutch tradition of sleeping in the first-floor rooms remained intact in this house for most of its existence.

SPOON RACK

The broad planes of Dutch houses, their smooth-plaster walls, planed deep beams, and wide floorboards, do not prepare the uninitiated for the sometimes intricate detail of small Dutch objects. The Netherlands spoon rack (*lepel bord*) was meant as a gift to a wife from her husband, a token of affection and an emblem of family unity. After meals members of the family deposited their spoons, the main utensil for eating, into his or her own slot. That tradition continued in the New World until the late eighteenth century. Most surviving racks are associated with Bergen County, New Jersey; they are carved as this one, often with initials and dates, and were brightly painted (this one was orange).

SOUTH ROOM ("OLD KITCHEN")

A later window in the door is one of the few alterations in this room, the "old kitchen," circa 1735. The desk was likely made in nearby Kingston, the only village of size that supported cabinetmakers. We know of the workshops of the Beekman and Elting families to whom several *kases*—and likely other joinery work like this desk—have been attributed. Simpler furniture, without joinery, could be made by farmers or local carpenters.

The Decker Barn

Wallkill, Ulster County, New York

Carefully restored in recent years, the Dutch three-aisle barn that Cornelis Decker likely built after the Revolution, was especially suited to the cash-crop wheat farming that the Dutch preferred. With the help of servants and slaves, an enterprising farmer could cultivate hundreds of acres and amass considerable wealth by shipping his grain to market in New York City and from there to other colonies, the Caribbean, and the Continent. New York was long known as the breadbasket of the colonies.

NAVE

Large anchor beams span the center aisle or nave, both to secure or "anchor" the columns which support the roof but also to hold a "flooring" of poles onto which wheat and hay could be stacked and ventilated. Wide doors and gable air holes also aided drying by facilitating air circulation; they were designed to preserve produce from rot and the barn from spontaneous combustion.

Fresh or wet hay was kept away from barns. If not dried properly it caused a chemical reaction when it rotted, generating enough heat to create spontaneous combustion and fire. Hay barracks were inexpensive to build and distanced a threat of fire from the valuable barn and its crop of grain—the major profit of a farm year.

GABLE

Pulled by two horses, a Dutch wagon filled with wheat entered the gable end of the barn, its produce raised onto the anchor beams and pole flooring above where air circulation could dry it. The "martin holes" in the upper gable facilitated air circulation. Small doors allowed livestock to enter stalls in the side aisles where they faced the large central aisle for convenient feeding. The pentice over the wagon doors helped to protect the sill beam from moisture since the ground was backed against it to form a ramp for the wagon wheels.

We are subjected to a trouble and expense to which, I am informed, you [in Europe] are wholly strangers, and that is to salt our cattle regularly once a week. . . . So great is the necessity of salting our cattle that they will all become wild, restless, and incapable of being kept within the bounds of our farms. . . . hardly give any milk . . .
—J. Hector St. John de Crevecoeur, Orange County, NY, 1782 [*Sketches*, p. 289]

The Jan Van Deusen House

Hurley, Ulster County, New York

Founded in 1663, Hurley was originally called New Dorp (New Village). Jan Van Deusen of Claverack (Columbia County) came here in 1719 to marry and soon after built this house. The house was progressive for this early date since it had a central hall. In 1777, the Van Deusen house briefly served as the meeting place of the Committee of Safety of the State of New York, in effect the "state capital." That was unique, but "Washington slept here" has probably led to the preservation of more houses than any other impulse.

FRONT OF HOUSE
(EXTERIOR)

Dutch houses are not just a product of tradition and materials. On the west side of the Hudson River in Ulster, Greene, and Albany counties stratified limestone was readily available and almost universally used for building. Most houses were laid up with rubble stone or irregular limestone. Some house builders elected to select and shape limestone into blocks, as with the Van Deusen house, creating a regularity of facade most appealing to Dutch sensibilities.

HALL

In our eyes the central hall is a "hallmark" of colonial homes. Yet it was not a feature of Dutch houses until the acceptance of the English house plan in the eighteenth century. Where once the Dutch door (and stoop) demarcated public from private spaces, now the hall served this function. In effect the outside, the public area of a Dutch house, was now brought into the house hall, but not into private rooms.

DOOR

Although widely known as "Dutch," split doors are found throughout Europe, although most favored in The Netherlands. Besides "keeping the pigs out and the kids in" they had other functions: admitting air and light into a hall or room, and allowing social and trade interaction while keeping privacy. Today it retains a sense of romance primarily for its oddity, not its usefulness. Our way of life is more English than Dutch; we no longer use the door to both beckon and withhold.

DINING ROOM

The passion for collecting antiques is not new, but the popularity of collecting has received much impetus from magazines and books. This view graced the cover of a national magazine, reflecting and inspiring countless others to adorn their rooms with antiques, collectibles, and decorative objects. Objects, like houses, are expressions of the owners' identity with the visual and historic; each object, like holiday ornaments, is associated with personal feelings, social relations, and aesthetic preferences. In time they fill a house as much as they fulfill our dreams.

BEDROOM DORMER

While the garrets of Dutch houses were once unfinished, they began to contain one or more bedrooms with a fireplace (later with just a stove) by the late eighteenth century. As rooms for habitation they also required more light and thus had dormers added, as pictured here; these date from the nineteenth century or later. The predilection to leave exposed rough-hewn rafters and collar beams is a colonial revival idea of the twentieth century, bringing out to view whatever original features still remained in early houses that had often undergone multiple modernizations, even restorations.

The Gomez Mill House

Marlboro, Ulster County, New York

Often overlooked among the welter of immigrant groups were Jews who came to New York seeking refuge and prosperity. As a boy, Louis Moses Gomez (1654–1740) fled with his family from the Spanish Inquisition. He found temporary refuge, and a wife, in France; then came to New York City before 1700. He received the right of "denization" which, as a Jew, allowed him to own land. In New York he established himself as a successful merchant and landowner. On a creek near the Hudson River in Ulster County he acquired six thousand nine hundred acres in 1714 and built a trading post, lumber mill, and lime kilns. The foundation of the present house is likely that of the original store.

EXTERIOR FRONT

Although the original trading post may date from about 1714, that part of the present structure which is above the original stone foundation dates from the period of Wolfert Acker's ownership, starting in 1772. The house once set into a hill, more recently removed, so that the main entrance was into the first floor at ground level. The opposite facade, seen here, has always been open to ground level entry to the cellar. The arched brick lintels over each window are an archaic survival of a much earlier Dutch building feature; the use of Flemish brick bond (alternating headers and streatchers in each course), however, is an up-to-date adaptation of a coming style much favored in the Federal period. Greek Revival windows of about 1830-40 are further evidence of a modernization process which this house has experienced throughout its life.

HEART AND DIAMOND

Most of this brick house dates from the tenure (1772–1799) of Wolfert Acker, a Dutchman who was active in the Revolution, but better known because of his grandfather's home in Tarrytown; Washington Irving turned it into his Sunnyside residence and wrote about it in *Wolfert's Roost*.

In a gable end a heart and diamond are set into the brickwork. Such motifs, including the date when construction was completed or the owner's initials, are to be found in other Dutch and Anglo-Dutch houses, expressing in brick, incised stone, or wrought iron ownership, pride, marriage, and/or achievement.

EUROPEAN CUPBOARD

The Gomez house has had a varied history reflected in extensive changes in structure and, in recent years, changes in furnishings by owners seeking to rekindle a connection to that past. An assortment of furniture expressing the hand craftsmanship of centuries ago now decorates the house, of which this early European cupboard is a distinctive example.

DINING ROOM

A mixture of objects from four centuries, all quite congenial in their juxtaposition, show how compatibility does not result just from similarity in period or style, but can be artfully derived from texture, color, use, and patina. The former is about restoration, the latter, about decoration; two approaches which today dominate the fixing up of old houses. On the cupboard a flickering Menorah stands as an emblem of the house's first owner—the only colonial house standing in New York with Jewish associations.

FIREBACK

Some relics of the past, by their very nature, disappear with use. Cast iron firebacks were once ubiquitous in colonial fireplaces. By their very function—to protect brick or stone—most were eventually consumed. A constant winter fire can destroy the back of a fireplace in a season unless protected by a fireback which can last two dozen years—or forever if used infrequently. With the advent of cast iron stoves, firebacks were no longer made although their ornamentation reprieved some from discard. This one was made by the Oxford Furnace in New Jersey in the 1750s, its British arms somehow escaping the usual rejection by Revolutionaries.

Besides the different sects of Christians, many Jews have settled in New York, who possess great privileges. They have a synagogue, own their dwelling-houses, possess large country-seats and are allowed to keep shops in town. They have likewise several ships, which they load and send out with their own goods. In fine, they enjoy all the privileges common to the other inhabitants of this town and province.
—Peter Kalm, 1749–50
[*Travels*, p. 129]

LARGE ROOM

The front cellar room of the present house was likely two rooms of the original Gomez trading post dating from about 1714. By the end of the 1700s, the house was extended into a large structure of later design. Today this part of the cellar is one large room; an early Netherlands chest and some animal pelts suggesting its original use, with other furnishings and a fireplace of another period.

DE HALVE MAEN (THE HALF MOON)

The stained glass image of Henry Hudson's ship *de Halve Maen* (The Half Moon) was the romantic product of Dard Hunter, a well-known paper and book maker and authority on the history of paper making who built a paper mill by the stream when he owned the property between 1913 and 1919. No doubt he was aware that on the river shore nearby, Henry Hudson observed Native Americans dancing and named the location *Dans Kamer* (the Dance Chamber), a name it still retains today. Such objective or linguistic emblems of Hudson River Valley history have been preserved by predecessors with forethought of our enduring fascination with the mysteries of our past.

The Cornelis Wynkoop House

Marbletown, Ulster County, New York

Along the road that traverses Stone Ridge is an imposing stone house; a deep valley can be seen at its rear. What is now the rear wing originally was a small Dutch house (twenty-nine by twenty-four feet) built in about 1718 when Lambent and Thomas Dolderbrink acquired title to five hundred seventy acres. It is similar in layout to others in the Marbletown region with two rooms; one has a Dutch fireplace and the other has an iron stove fed through the wall by the adjacent fireplace. Such modest stone houses were built in great numbers in this region of Ulster County and a remarkable number survive today.

The house passed through two owners before being acquired by Cornelis E. Wynkoop at the time of his marriage to Cornelia Mancius in 1766. He set about improving the property by building a large house (sixty by twenty-four feet) onto the old house, which now became the kitchen. Wynkoop was evidently a prosperous merchant and farmer who also served as surveyor of the highway (1774–83), overseer of the poor (1777), town supervisor (1777–82), justice of the peace (1782), and, during the Revolution, as third in command of the Ulster County Regiment under Aaron Burr and George Clinton. However, his lasting fame derives from the fact that General Washington spent the night here on November 15, 1782 on his way to Kingston to give a speech. The unaltered condition of this house, like many others, owes much to the awe with which subsequent generations have held Washington and all things associated with him.

GABLE (NORTH FRONT AND EAST)

In any community there is at least one house which stands out because of size and design—a product of one individuals taste, wealth, and ambition. Eschewing more land or slaves, Wynkoop chose to spend more money on an expansive house, a New Style house that was two-stories high with upstairs bedrooms and fireplaces. It was unlike the dozens of other stone houses nearby—traditional Dutch story-and-a-half types. If Wynkoop desired to create or confirm his status, his new house became a self-fulfilling prophecy when it was selected as Washington's overnight accommodation.

WEST GABLE
AND ADDITION

The original house became the kitchen wing, used mostly in summer when its excess fireplace heat could be kept outside the main house. Such small houses had two habitation rooms (three if they had a cellar fireplace). When New Style houses or additions were built, they were only a half-story higher. But with habitation on the second floor, the increase in usable space went from two or three rooms to as many as eleven rooms, thus vastly increasing and changing the lifestyle of the family.

GARDEN

Nestled into the back corner nook of the Wynkoop house is a revival of a seventeenth-century boxwood garden. Such gardens were found in New Amsterdam (New York City) and were likely found elsewhere in the colonial period as well; all traces have long since vanished though. They were especially suitable close to the house where one could view the full splendor of their intricate designs from a window above.

The center hall is unusually wide, accommodating an equally unusual stairway set forward of the back wall (thus giving access to the rear right room) and extending two flights to the garret. The innovation of the hallway gave rooms greater personal privacy as well as protection from seasonal temperature extremes.

EAST FRONT BEDROOM

When Anglo-Dutch (Georgian) houses began to be built a full two stories high it was to accommodate family members in their own bedrooms with a new level of comfort. Spacious second floor rooms permitted fireplaces and cupboards within paneled walls, features heretofore on the first floor.

In 1838 this bedroom and the living room below were painted white, about the only decorating change this house has ever undergone. Originally the woodwork of this room was painted blue-gray, a popular color in Dutch houses.

LIVING ROOM (NORTHWEST)

The principal parlor has changed as little as the rest of the house. Once painted red, the most common color used in early Dutch houses, the woodwork was painted green before the end of the eighteenth century, the most common color in Georgian houses of the same region. Until a few years ago, many of the original furnishings of the house remained unchanged as well.

REAR SITTING ROOM (WEST)

On the right side of the house, this small rear sitting room shares a partition-wall chimney with the larger dining room in front. Originally painted a red-brown, the green second coat has been untouched for so long that swords hung over the fireplace left a shadow, inspiring their replacements. Unseen beyond the fireplace is a corner cupboard and an entry to the dining room.

GARRET

The feeling of a house as it originally was is likely to be found in its most remote part. The upper garret is where the darkened color of aging wood in itself evokes the sense that time has stood still for centuries. Three garret levels suggest ample room for storage yet only one was used. The rows of extra bracing indicate that this complex structure had more to do with strength and stability against wind and snow loads than with a need for space.

CELLAR VIEW (FROM EAST TO WEST TO DOORWAY)

The cellars of today are often forgotten storage areas, but on a self-sufficient subsistence farm of the pre-Revolutionary period, it was more actively used than some of the upstairs rooms. If there was a kitchen in the cellar, it was finished almost as carefully as the rooms above, with smooth planed beams and ceiling boards, cupboards, mantles, and floorboards. Consumables were stored in a ventilated slatted pantry (*left*), protected from pilfering by a locked door. Beyond is an arch support for the parlor fireplace above and, to the right of the exterior door, the kitchen fireplace, actively used in cold weather when its warmth was welcome in the rooms above.

DOOR LOCKS (CELLAR)

Locks on doors were ubiquitous in colonial America. They were not only found on exterior doors, as today, but on interior doors and furniture too. Reasons which inspired such a sense of insecurity included: living as most did on a frontier near real or imagined enemies, being largely unprotected by the force of law, and being surrounded by the unsure loyalty of neighbors, transients, servants, and slaves.

The Philipsburg Manor

Tarrytown, Westchester County, New York
Historic Hudson Valley, Inc., Tarrytown, New York

Philipsburg Manor House was the center of a milling
and trading complex founded by Frederick Philipse
(1626–1702) on his fifty-two-thousand-acre manorial
grant. The structure was built in about 1680 and enlarged
by his son in the early eighteenth century. It was a domicile
but also administrative center, warehouse, and commercial
dairy surrounded by a mill, wharf, slave house, and bake
house, among other buildings.

BARN INTERIOR

Cows, horses, and sometimes sheep, found
shelter within Dutch barns, especially in
winter. Farms were scattered over the landscape, often far from towns, so each needed
to be self-sufficient. Besides a family, a prosperous farmer may have had hired hands
and/or slaves who were responsible for
much of the farm work. The three-aisle
structure of Dutch barns was suitable for
crop farming and subsistence animal hus-
bandry, the wide center aisle for receiving,
storing, and processing the former, the side
aisles for the latter, which entered by side
doors. This might be the last Dutch barn to
demonstrate its full use.

BARN

Dutch barns have the spiritual quality of a cathedral in the wilderness. Indeed both derive from the same source—the medieval cloister barn—with three aisles, a high loft, and a symmetrical entrance in the gable end. Such barns were essential to Dutch farms, which were primarily crop farms with livestock only sufficient for domestic needs.

Beyond the kitchen garden and the barn were orchards. On the farms fields of corn, wheat, barley, oats, rye, squash, peas, pumpkins, and more were cultivated. Wheat and peas were the big commercial crops, and were shipped to New York City and beyond.

The farms were commonly built close to the river, on the hills. Each house had a little kitchen garden and a still lesser orchard. Some farms, however, had large gardens. The kitchen gardens yielded several kinds of pumpkins, watermelon and kidney beans.
—Peter Kalm, 1749–50 [*Travels*, p. 335]

KITCHEN GARDEN

From the very beginning of settlement, the Dutch cultivated gardens. The kitchen garden was conveniently close to the house, laid out in raised beds in the ancient manner. Here herbs (medicinal, culinary, and for dyes), vegetables, and flowers were all tended by the lady of the house. This applied to both rural and urban houses, although the more prosperous among the latter also favored ornamental gardens. A bird's-eye view of New Amsterdam in about 1660 shows many such gardens set out in hedged boxes and circles.

Mount Gulian, Verplanck–Van Wyck Barn

Beacon, Dutchess County, New York
Mt. Gulian Historic Site, Verplanck Homestead, Beacon, New York

On a farm and mill site along the course of Sprout Creek in southern Dutchess County, Philip Verplanck, Jr. built a handsome brick Anglo-Dutch house in 1768. Likely it was he who also built this Dutch barn about the same time. The farm remained in the Verplanck family until 1827 when it was sold to Richard C. Van Wyck in whose family it remained for generations. In recent years this distinctive barn was re-erected at Mt. Gulian, a related Verplanck homestead which is now a museum.

ANCHOR BEAM AND POST

Dutch barns were adapted primarily for crop framing and secondarily for domestic stock. Wheat, a staple commercial crop throughout the Hudson Valley, was off-loaded from wagons onto the barn loft above where it dried before being brought to the floor for threshing. The anchor beams, as seen here, were made especially large to bear the weight of these crops.

Opening doors at either end of the spacious central aisle allowed wind to pass though; this aided in winnowing the grain from its chaff. The grain was then bagged and taken to the mill or sent to market, usually in New York City.

. . . to build a barn . . . with an opening on both sides; the barn shall be 60 feet long and 30 feet broad with a floor of timber (balke), horse crib, cow stall and loft (solder) therin, shortened to fifty feet in length and of the breadth of the barn; on condition that harme aforesaid shall furnish them victuals and drink, and all the timber, and deliver the materials that belong thereto on the ground; . . . for which he, Harme Gansevoort, promises to pay the sum of forty beavers. —Contract to build a barn for Harme Gansevoort at Catskill, November 29, 1677

GABLE

Few Dutch barns from the pre-Revolutionary period survive, but this is one of them. Like others, it has a high roof but low sides. This one is notable for its unusual, but not unique, cantilevered gables extending out eighteen inches. Its outline replicates the entire gable's shape, a pleasing artifice going beyond its likely function—overhanging protection from rain for the entryway.

The Daniel De Klerck House
(later the John DeWint House)

Tappan, Rockland County, New York
DeWint House at Tappan, New York, The Grand Lodge
of Free and Accepted Masons of the State of New York

Daniel De Klerck emigrated from Oostberg, The Netherlands to New York in about 1676. He married the widow of a patentee of lands acquired from the Tappan Indians and led a group to settle there in 1686–87. His first home may have been a small wing on the present house but it was removed in about 1850. A man of leadership, De Klerck was magistrate, militia captain, and a member of the Committee of Safety in 1689. In 1700 he built the present stone and brick house on his two-hundred-acre farm, proudly emblazoning the date in brick across the front.

When Daniel De Klerck died in 1731, the farm was sold to settle his estate. In 1746 it was purchased by John DeWint of New York City who gave it historical prominence by hosting General Washington on four occasions between 1780 and 1783 and later, entertaining British General Carlton at the end of the Revolution. In the nineteenth century it had several owners but was then purchased by the Grand Lodge of Free and Accepted Masons of the State of New York, in commemoration of General Washington, a member of that fraternal order. It has been a museum ever since and is called the George Washington Masonic Historic Site at Tappan, New York. A kitchen wing has been added to replace the one demolished in the 1850s.

GABLE

De Klerck's house is unusual for its place and time, being mostly of brick in a region where stone houses predominate and having a steep pitch roof. By this early time, most Dutch houses in the lower Hudson River Valley had lower roofs. The extended eaves, however, are in keeping with the house's own region. Likely there were other such houses now long gone which displayed this conservative Netherlandish quality in the regions around New York City. Its preservation is likely another example of the influence of George Washington's presence.

DELFTWARE TILES

Delftware tiles in manganese (purple) or in blue that depicted stories from the Bible were the most popular fireplace decorations on both Dutch and English fireplaces from the seventeenth through the eighteenth centuries. In The Netherlands, where most were made, they were used to cover the entire back of a Dutch fireplace, even entire walls. In America such extravagance was usually limited to one or two columns of tiles on a Dutch fireplace wall, although so many were reused on this fireplace it suggests that the back of the original Dutch fireplace was all tiled.

PARLOR FIREPLACE

The main room of the house, to the right of the center hall, was built with a Dutch fireplace, the mantle molding of which was retained when the space below was enclosed with an English fireplace and paneling, likely after DeWint acquired the house in 1746. Biblical tiles and two wood pilasters from the old fireplace were reset on the new surface, thus successfully accommodating old features while updating to the newer style fireplace.

The Gidney House

Newburgh, Orange County, New York

Eliazer Gidney is believed to be the original owner of this house. Of English descent, he may be related to one Eliazer Gidney who was living in Salem, Massachusetts, in 1670 (A Bartholomew Gidney was one of the magistrates in the Salem witch trials of 1692). If so, and for whatever reason, an Eliazer Gidney chose to settle in the Hudson Valley. The house's structure and details suggest a date of about 1760. While appearing to be a conventional Dutch house on the exterior, on the interior it laid out as a New England plan, appropriate to the apparent background of its owner.

GABLE EXTERIOR

While appearing to be a house of the southern Dutch region with its long extended eaves, this house is, in fact, in the mid-Hudson River valley, near Newburgh. Its interior is equally incongruent to its exterior for within the front door one sees a New England house: dogleg stairway and a central fireplace stack with three fireplaces for a parlor and a dining room in the front, and kitchen across the back.

WINDOW DETAIL (ENGRAVED NAME)

A pane of early green window glass once succumbed to an urge to let others know that this inscriber was once here. The glass in early houses was imported "crown" glass, blown in a large bubble then spun to a round sheet which was cut into rectangles or diamonds, the round center piece of thicker glass, known as the crown, being used for small round door windows. The color of the glass depended on the impurities of the sand, and shades of green were common.

RED DOOR

A surface undisturbed for centuries is a rarity. Most houses have undergone many changed in paint schemes but, more recently, restorations to early colors are popular. Yet today such original surfaces receive the greatest encomiums for their rarity and for the richness of their patina. This small door gives access to the cellar stairway from the hall. A compass-inscribed decorative circle on the door is a mechanical doodle found occasionally on other early woodwork, more likely the product of children's or carpenters' play than any intended occult hex sign (although there was concern among colonists about the malevolent powers of others, well expressed in the many folk tales of the Dutch region).

SMOKE HOUSE

Near many Dutch farm houses once stood small smoke houses; these were essential to the preservation of meats, giving them flavor and slowing the depredation of flies and rot. Like the majority of farm structures they have mostly disappeared from the landscape. A complete farm had most or all of the following features: a house; kitchen house (attached or not); bake oven (attached or not); large three-aisle barn and barn yard; small one-aisle or nave barn (wagon shed); one or more hay barracks; hog pen; chicken house; shop (tools, weaving loom, forge, and so on); corn crib; sheep fold; smoke house; root cellar (in the cellar or separate); and bee houses. Add to these the dozens of types of implements and tools, and perhaps servants and slaves, and a family was ready to live off the land.

CORNER CABINET

Although this is a house made for a New Englander, the craftsmen who built this house were trained in the Dutch manner which shows in other features such as the parallel smooth-planed Dutch beams. This legacy of training is also revealed in more recent restorations of early houses wherein craftsmen, despite trying to copy features exactly, inadvertently reveal traces of their own modernism, often not recognized as such until years later. Time is a great revealer.

KITCHEN WING

To the left of the house front is a small one-room wing traditionally thought to be the original house built by Eliazer Gidney, purportedly made by him in Sawpits, Westchester County and reassembled here on the thirteen hundred acres he had purchased in the early eighteenth century. However, its structure (planed and beaded ceiling boards and beams, the latter small, and an English fireplace), would suggest it is the more conventional kitchen addition, dating from the late eighteenth century. Its unaltered state retains the cozy feeling that must have appealed to the Gidneys long ago.

The Abraham Storms–
Capt. Larry Sneden House

Sneden's Landing, Palisades, New York

Few Dutch houses overlook the Hudson River, for most were farm houses oriented to creek flatlands in the interior. An exception is the stone and wood house built by Abraham Storms just after the Revolution. Little is known of Storms but his successor was Capt. Lawrence Sneden (1800–1871) who acquired the house in 1834 and operated a ferry that crossed the river at what became known as Sneden's Landing. He was also a shipbuilder and state assemblyman. Hudson River "landings" were once the hub of commerce between Albany and New York City. Almost all farm produce and manufactured products went by boat from landing to landing. Up until 1850, when the railroad arrived, the river bustled with boat traffic and after Fulton's successful steamboat (1809), with churning paddlewheels.

REAR EXTERIOR FACADE

Most of our visible heritage is contained primarily in farm houses which have survived two and three centuries, not only because they are historic but because they are so adaptable to changing lifestyles. Despite all the new utilities, innovative appliances, and lifestyle changes, old houses keep readapting successfully. If old houses lose much of their authenticity in the renovation it is usually because too much money was spent, not too little. Even when extensively renovated, as pictured here, early houses can still inspire a renewed feeling for the past—especially when they have boxwood gardens and espalier trees.

LIVING ROOM AND MANTLE

We know a house is not a home until shared dreams are lovingly mixed in. The accouterments of that dream may consist of a fireplace, a comfortable lounge chair, good reading books, and a view. For generations, the Hudson River Valley has been the weekend dream of countless New York urbanites seeking to restore their spirits. However altered or furnished, old country houses have retained this charm since Washington Irving's time.

DINING ROOM

Old houses are expressions of both themselves and of their owners; the more they express their past owners, the less they have left to express their original selves. Yet for many the lure of the past is irresistible, inspiring restoration and creative decoration to bring back a feeling of the past while giving new life to a once neglected or renovated house.

BEDROOM

Once an open garret, this second-floor space became a habitable room when improved heating systems made it comfortable. All features have long since been modernized, except for the hood chimney of what had been a Dutch fireplace in the room below.

CUPBOARD DOOR

What we call American folk art has its roots in Europe where ethnic groups, peasant cultures, and bourgeoisie created ornamental designs and emblematic meanings on their possessions, often derived from the aristocracy in those hierarchical societies. As one scholar said, "folk art is the fallen culture of the upper class." The idealized folk maiden on a dower cupboard or chest, while European, is appealing to Americans whose ancestral ties have become fragmented by time and distance.

The Islands and the Jerseys
Long Island, Staten Island, and New Jersey

Kings and Queens Counties (Western Long Island)

New Netherland's original claim to territory extended from Hartford (in what is now Connecticut) to Swanendael, now Lewis, Delaware. A colony or its host nation, however, can hold only what it can secure regardless of claims. Realistically the Dutch culture area came to mean just the Hudson River Valley, the westernmost edge of Long Island, and parts of New Jersey. This is where the Dutch settled in sufficient numbers to secure their claim, at least temporarily. Manhattan was the first place settled, but within a year families were acquiring land from the Native Americans on the western edge of Long Island, a short row or sail from New Amsterdam (New York City) across the East River. Despite this water barrier, the flat meadows, forests, and inlets of what we now call Brooklyn were so inviting that this region became, in effect, the first suburb. Five Dutch towns (and one English—Gravesend) were quickly founded on lands acquired from the Canarsie Indians: New Amersfoort (Flatlands); Breukelen (Brooklyn); Midwout (Flatbush); New Utrecht; and Woodtown (Bushwick) were the beginnings of a continual and prosperous expansion resulting in Kings County becoming about the wealthiest area in New York.

Just north of Kings County was and still is Queens County. This area was primarily settled by New Englanders except at the north edge of Kings County, along the Newtown Creek and directly opposite Manhattan, where some Dutch took up lands. One Dutch town was created in 1645, at Vlissing or Flushing. Still other Dutchmen settled along the East River in sheltering bays. The last surviving Dutch houses in Queens County were to be found in Newtown and shared the same features found in those in Kings County.

The attractiveness of the land and the prosperity of the settlers in Kings County is reflected in the houses they built over the next century and more. As elsewhere, first settlers began with the crudest of shelters. More permanent houses quickly followed although the very prosperity of the region in the twentieth century caused nearly all traces of these early houses to be obliterated by development. We know from a nine-teenth-century illustration that Klaes Arents Vechte built an impressive house at Gowanus in 1699. It was a full two-story stone and brick Dutch house with a steep pitch roof and parapet gables. In design it was similar to houses built in New Amsterdam and not unlike others that survive in the Albany region. If this was once a style of house to be found in Brooklyn, other records of them have been lost except for the Jan Martense Schenck house (1675) once at Mill Island, Flatlands, and now in the Brooklyn Museum. It is a wood house but otherwise was built with a steep pitch roof over two rooms, not unlike some that also survive in the Albany area.

What does survive in drawings, photographs, and a few existing houses in Brooklyn is another type of house entirely, the one-and-a-half-story wood house with lower pitch roof and, in most cases, eaves extending out from the body of the house in the front (and sometimes in the back). Some of these have been traditionally dated as early as the 1650s, possibly earlier, such as the Wyckoff house (p. 189). If so, they represent a significant architectural design innovation in New Netherland, the first break from the decidedly Netherlands-type house built in the colony's cities and, if the Vechte and Schenck represent a nearly lost type, on farms in Brooklyn and in the upper Hudson River Valley. Why this different type was developed, that is, how it can be accounted for in terms of historical prototypes and practical and social functions, has not been satisfactorily explained. Some have thought it was a French innovation, pointing to such extended eaves on houses in Quebec and earlier, in Normandy, France. There were Huguenot settlers in Brooklyn as elsewhere but this type of house is not specifically linked to them.

Richmond County (Staten Island)

Staten Island encloses the west side of New York Harbor as Brooklyn encloses the east side, creating one of the great natural harbors of the world, one of the most appealing features to the seafaring Dutch. Only after a 1660 treaty with the Indians was concluded did successful settlement begin. In 1661 a group of Dutch and French formed the community of Oude Dorp (Old Town). After Richmond County was created in 1683 (along with the establishment

Previous page: As in their houses, the New World Dutch developed regional variations in furnishings. While the Dutch cupboard or kas was ubiquitous, in Bergen County a distinctive cupboard or dresser with glass doors, now known as a Hackensack cupboard, evolved after the

Revolution. More English than Dutch in form, it had a variety of decorative features applied or incised which appealed to the Dutch. Also in Bergen County there was a preference for intricately carved spoonracks, a Netherlands form which remained unchanged here until 1800.

of all other counties) additional towns were founded on the island. The governor then gave out numerous small patents and several manors to encourage further development. Besides the Dutch and French Walloons, a variety of people came here including English, Waldensians, and Moravians.

For centuries Staten Island lagged behind other boroughs of New York City in development and as a consequence more early houses survive here than elsewhere. Some of these houses have been brought together for further preservation at Richmond Town Restoration. It was not until the eighteenth century that the New Style home began to be built here, with pitch or gambrel roofs, the latter associated with increasing number of rooms necessitating deeper houses.

NEW JERSEY

Bergen County

Dutch habitation of what is now Bergen County met with Indian hostility until Governor Stuyvesant bought the land from its original inhabitants in 1658. As an added precaution he required all settlers to live in palisaded villages. In 1660 the village of Bergen was established at what is now Jersey City and as elsewhere, a Dutch Church was organized shortly thereafter. Effective settlement awaited English conquest and the beginning of proprietorship under James Carteret. He actively granted tracts to individuals, groups, and speculators creating a veritable quilt of small and large parcels sold on attractive terms to those who were delighted to bypass the leasehold manors in New York. Like New York, New Jersey counties were established in 1682/3, Bergen County being initially a small area along the shore. Later it was expanded to the west and still later contracted somewhat to its present size. The earliest settlements were at Old Hackensack (now Ridgefield Park); subsequent communities developed at Paramus, Saddle River, Teaneck, New Bridge, River Edge, Schraalenburg, Closter, Old Tappan, Tenafly, Hasbrouck Heights, and elsewhere.

Almost without exception the houses of Bergen County were constructed of widely available red sandstone. The

early houses used rough stones; the later ones had neatly dressed stonework on the front, with sides and rear walls getting this treatment later on. This created a shorthand way to date construction. Some have pitch roofs, steeper in the early period, but a majority have gambrel roofs, usually associated as elsewhere with houses two-rooms deep. Most of these have the same overhanging eaves first seen in Kings County.

The initiation of the extended eave in Bergen County appears to date from the late seventeenth century and continued in popularity for a long period, well into the nineteenth century. Such a long period of popularity for any architectural feature suggests not only practical efficiency but also aesthetic desirability. The generally accepted beauty of the sweeping extended eave combined with the gambrel roof is still with us today. This type of house, regardless of its non-Dutch origins (neither feature is found in The Netherlands), has come to define in the average person's mind what a Dutch house is in the United States.

It is in Bergen County that this type of house achieved its ultimate and extreme form with overhangs extending out several feet; some later owners attached porch posts in fear of the extended eave's apparent instability.

Monmouth County

From the time of its first settlement, Monmouth County had a close connection to those who lived in western Long Island (today's Brooklyn). The first purchase from the Native Americans was by English from Gravesend in 1663, followed by the large Monmouth Patent of 1665 that included all of the present county plus parts of adjacent counties. Englishmen (Baptists and Quakers) from Long Island began to settle around what is now Middletown and Shrewsbury. In 1682–83, Scots took up land at Freehold and finally, in 1690 and 1695, a number of Dutch from Long Island and New York City arrived. At Holmdel the Couwenhovens, Schencks, and Hendricksons built homes of which only a few survive. They show relationships to some Long Island houses (p. 48, 197), such as the use of shingle siding, extended eaves, and on the earlier houses, steep pitch roofs.

Middlesex County

Adjacent to Monmouth County, Middlesex County was first patented in 1664 to Englishmen from Long Island and they along with Scots became the predominant residents of this county. Some Dutch later moved to the banks of the Raritan River. Here the town of New Brunswick—part Dutch, part English—was established. It was then in Somerset County. A Dutch church was founded in 1703 and the community received a city charter in 1730. Among the early residents were family names associated with Albany.

Somerset County

Although inland from the coast, Somerset County became home to a substantial number of Dutch for a reason that becomes obvious when the topography of the land is examined. Beginning in 1681, extensive land purchases were made from the Native Americans including broad fertile plains along the Raritan River. Soon after, other purchases were made along the Millstone River resulting in Dutch farms stretching along the banks of these rivers in and around Somerville (formerly Raritan), Bound Brook, Millstone, Middlebush, Franklin Park (then Six Mile Run), Belle Mead, and Harlingen.

Primarily wood houses are to be found in this county; some are sheathed in shingles and others in weatherboards. Far fewer are stone. Pitch roofs predominate and the overhanging eave is to be found on a small minority of houses.

Western New Jersey

Where good land could be obtained Dutchmen migrated, even into the interior parts of New Jersey, a region primarily inhabited by the English, especially Quakers. Passaic County was mostly populated by Dutch who migrated westward from Bergen County. South and east of Bergen County is Essex County which received Dutch settlers in its northern half, the English being in the other part. The boundaries of these three adjacent counties were much altered over the centuries so it is difficult to describe settlement patterns by this designation. Of the houses built in Passaic and Essex Counties, almost all are stone and have gable roofs; only those once in Bergen County have overhanging eaves.

Present day Hunterdon County is to the west of Somerset and borders the Delaware River, the western boundary of New Jersey. This region was settled by Quakers and Germans from adjacent Pennsylvania. A few Dutchmen navigated up the Raritan River to buy farms around Readington, Pleasant Run, Three Bridges, Stanton, and Whitehorse—all in the eastern most part of the county. Their houses were of stone, with the use of brick as arched lintels.

Morris County is north of Somerset and Hunterdon, and west of Essex. It was acquired by a variety of land speculators and sold to farmers of different origins, including some Dutch in Pequanock township in the northeast, primarily at Pompton and Pompton Plains. These communities are in the northeast corner bordering Passaic, Bergen, and Essex Counties. Of these houses, most are stone with steep pitch roofs. They tend to be small and lack the stylish extended eaves or gambrel roofs common in Bergen County.

Sussex and Warren Counties make up the very northwest portion of New Jersey—west of Passaic and Morris Counties, south of the New York border, and east of the Delaware River. This was accessible to New York Dutch via the Rondout and Neversink Valleys by the Old Mine Road that extended from Kingston through Ulster County to Port Jervis on the Delaware River. In the 1690s Dutch and Huguenots came and settled in the Neversink Valley in New York and then in the Minisink region, the valley of the Delaware River above and below the Delaware Water Gap.

The houses of this region appear more like those of Ulster County than those elsewhere in New Jersey even though, as the crow flies, they were closer to other New Jersey Dutch settlements. Of stone, either limestone or sandstone, with steep pitch roofs and no overhanging eaves, they were indeed frontier structures suitable to this isolated region still on the fringes of Indian county in the eighteenth century. Some do have a feature that is typical of houses in western New Jersey, a slightly rounded lintel of stone over windows.

The Pieter Claessen Wyckoff House
Canarsie Lane, Flatlands, Kings County, New York
New York City Department of Parks and Recreation
and the Wyckoff House & Association Inc.

This house would seem to date from the eighteenth century with its center hall and two-room-deep configuration. In fact it has a well documented ownership by Pieter Claessen (Wyckoff is a surname he added to conform to a later English law) who began residence here in 1655. Claessen either built the house or moved into it; it could have been built as early as 1638. If so, it is the oldest surviving house from New Netherland. Pieter Claessen left an enviable record of achievement. He arrived in Albany in 1637, a young illiterate indentured servant from East Friesland (now in Germany) and worked himself up to becoming the wealthiest inhabitant of New Amersfoort (Flatlands) on Long Island. He died in 1694 and was buried under the pulpit of his Dutch church.

WINDOW FRAME

This house underwent extensive changes in the eighteenth century, including the insertion of a center hall and rear rooms. The latter necessitated moving back the roof line to re-center it. As a result the chimney stacks of the front-room fireplaces were corbeled at a dramatic angle to meet the new apex, showing once again how the main features of a house—room arrangement, fireplaces, and roof-line chimneys— are closely interconnected and how changes in one affect the others.

Within the old walls the remains of a casement window frame survive from the earliest period, circa 1655, possibly earlier. In a later alteration, the frame was in-filled with slats of wood around which clay was packed to form airtight walls covered with plaster and whitewash. This kind of in-filling created a dense wall mass which acted as insulation against cold or heat, moderating the extremes of seasonal temperature.

FRONT

Like an abstract face, the kitchen wing of the Wyckoff house stares blankly from under its early roof out onto modern Brooklyn. Wedged between a fast food emporium and a junkyard, its one acre of green is just enough to suggest the large farm that once claimed all the land for blocks around. The house's recent experience was eerily prefigured by Pieter Claessen's own rags to riches life. Three

centuries to the day he stepped ashore, descendants organized the Wyckoff Family Association in America to save the now derelict house described by Joyce Kilmer as:

Yea, it hurts to look at the slanting roof
And the shingles falling apart.
For I can't help thinking the Wyckoff House
Is a house with a broken heart.

INTERIOR

Art imitating art. The United States and The Netherlands share the innovation of democracy and not surprisingly, a delight in the life of the common man. This may explain our affinity for Dutch Old Master paintings of domestic scenes. When those sunlit settings occur within our own Dutch houses, the resemblance to paintings by Vermeer, de Witt, de Hooch, and others is striking, evoking in us, as no doubt for early Wyckoff housewives, a visceral pleasure orchestrated by the play of subtle light on contrasting surfaces and colors.

The landlady called for the bedpan. I could not guess what she intended to do with it, unless it was to warm her bed to go to sleep after dinner; but I found that it was used by way of a chafing-dish to warm our dish of clams.
—Dr. Alexander Hamilton, Albany, 1744
[*Itinerarium*, p. 46]

KAS

As in The Netherlands, the American *kas*, or cupboard, was a ubiquitous form in Dutch houses serving the same purposes, yet showing regional variations in details, much as Dutch houses do. This example is typical of a group identified with Queens and western Nassau County (around Hempstead). Compared to the more boldly Netherlandish *kases* made in Kings County (Brooklyn), Manhattan, and the Hudson Valley (especially Kingston), this group has thinner and flatter moldings suggesting the influence of New England cabinetmaking, not surprising as these *kasen* come from a part of Long Island extensively settled by New Englanders. The *kas* was also made in southwestern Connecticut and shows even more of this trend.

The Minne Schenck House

Old Bethpage Village, Nassau County, New York
Nassau County Department of Recreation and Parks,
Old Bethpage Village Restoration

The Schenck family first arrived in New Amersfoort
(Flatlands) on Long Island in the 1650s. Jan Martense
Schenck is remembered for his 1664 house, now preserved
in the Brooklyn Museum. His brother Roelof became Kings
County Sheriff in 1685 and his two sons, like many on
Long Island, migrated to Monmouth County, New Jersey.
A younger son, Minne (1700–67) bought land for a farm at
Cow Neck (Manhasset), Long Island, and built this house
circa 1723–30, it remained in the family for nearly two centuries. By his death in 1767 Minne left a prosperous estate
including three slaves, "my clock and my large Dutch Bible,
and my writing-desk, and my iron back plate fireback, and
my bed with all its furniture fabrics . . ."

SHINGLED WALL

Wooden shingles on Dutch houses are a
New World innovation, a product of the
near limitless supply of suitable wood, both
for roofing and siding. As with so many
features of Dutch houses, whatever was utilitarian was expressed decoratively. Here
siding shingles are rounded, creating a
rhythmic pattern to a side wall. Likewise, the
Dutch felt that bright-colored paint was
both functional and decorative—preserving
wood against the elements, providing a
uniformity of color to emphasize the shape
of the shingles, and giving the viewer a
visually exciting color experience. The richly
saturated colors used by the Dutch, often as
many as three or four on a structure or feature, has only recently been rediscovered.

GABLE

Minne Schenck's house is large, thirty-nine-feet wide and thirty-two-feet deep, with two big square rooms in front and three narrow ones behind, all under a gentle pitch roof. Within a generation the house underwent a conventional evolution. It was widened ten feet to accommodate a center hall, disposing of separate doors to the two front rooms and opening the second floor to habitation.

Two gable-end Dutch fireplaces were replaced by English jambed fireplaces. A common feature of wood-sided Dutch houses was the exposure of the fireplace back wall to the open. While it presents a visual interruption of a harmonious facade, it insured that the hottest part of a fireplace would not ignite siding just inches away.

KAS

The *kas* is the most distinctive of Dutch furniture pieces in New York and New Jersey. Each region's cabinetmakers tended to certain characteristics such as their own moldings and panel forms.

BED BOX

In the front room on the left, evidence of a Dutch bed box was found during the restoration, inspiring this one. As no original bed box survived to the twentieth century, restorations are conjectural in detail, but the size and function is consistent with their use in The Netherlands which continued until the twentieth century. The benefit of such a bed, preheated by a bed warmer, was primarily to allow the occupant's body and respiration heat to be retained, warding off the increasing cold of a room as the hearth fire died during the night. Although alien to modern ideas, in those days the night air was considered bad for the health and curtains or doors acted as a defense.

PARLOR

When the house was reconfigured in the
period between 1740–60, the gable fireplace
in the front room to the right was removed
and a new, English-style back-to-back fireplace was placed on the partition wall, providing heat to two rooms with one chimney.
A mixture of old and up-to-date furniture
expresses the Dutch-English cultural
evolution taking place in New York and
New Jersey in the mid-eighteenth century.

The Jacob Adriance House

Flushing, Queens County, New York
New York City Department of Parks and Recreation
and Colonial Farmhouse Restoration Society of Bellerose

Jacob Adriance was a third generation family member to live on this farm when he acquired much of it at the time of his marriage and built this house in about 1772. It was at first framed in the Dutch manner but its plan was unusual—two-rooms deep with a side hall, more likely the result of Adriance's modest need for room—he and his wife did not have children—than because of the influence of the many New Englanders who settled in the Flushing area. In 1926 this last farm plot in Queens County was acquired by Creedmore Hospital; the house was preserved and recently became a museum.

REAR WINDOW (LEFT ROOM)

A lone surviving original window in the parlor looks out on a portion of the original farmstead which had been the last farm in Queens County—essentially unchanged for centuries.

GABLE

Adriance and his wife did not expand the house as almost all others did. Not until the 1840s was a balancing pair of rooms added to create a center-hall house. An insight into why such houses as this were expanded comes from John Bowne's three (successive) wives and six children who inspired multiple expansions of his Queens County home. As his first daughter-in-law put it ruefully, *"[the house] . . . was not wide an uf [enough] for my husband and his father, hee [sic] many times thretnes [sic, threatens] to turn us out of his house . . . ."* Peace was soon restored by an addition subsequent to the father's death (and his young widow's dismissal).

REAR ROOM

When the house was expanded in the 1840s its front entrance was moved from the north side to the south side. On entering the house today the first room is the original kitchen on the left, the room behind a parlor with a small bedroom beyond the fireplace, part of the partition wall still remains. Dividing off a small bedroom on the first floor is the first step after the original kitchen/parlor plan of earlier Dutch houses, the beginning of the evolution to privacy later culminating in second-floor bedrooms.

FRONT ROOM

From the hall a door opens into the kitchen, which has an English fireplace on the partition wall separating the room from the parlor (as well as a small bedroom) behind, whose fireplace was backed against the kitchen fireplace. There is evidence that this room first had a corner fireplace and that the present pair of partition-wall fireplaces soon replaced it as it was an efficient way of providing heat to both rooms using only one chimney. Early cupboards and paneling on either side of the fireplaces partially survive. The door displays the original blue-gray color of the interior.

Dutch Barn and Hay Barrack

Old Bethpage Village, Nassau County, New York
Old Bethpage Village Restoration

The probable builder and owner of this hay barrack was John Rogers Duryea of Muttontown, Long Island. He apparently had a nostalgic interest in his Dutch ancestry for he helped compile a genealogy of Long Island Dutch families. When he built this barrack, in about 1900, its function had passed except as a symbol of the vanishing ways of his farming ancestors. Hay barracks were once as plentiful as barns in the Dutch colonial regions, even into the end of the nineteenth century. As dairy farming overtook wheat growing as the staple of farms, hay has since been stored in barns and now outside in rolled bales.

In the background is an earlier Dutch barn, although its basic form is nearly timeless. Like the hay barrack, it is now preserved at Old Bethpage Village. The barn came from the Mohawk River Valley east of the town of Sharon in upstate New York.

In the colonial period when grain farming was paramount, hay was stored in hay barracks (*hooiberg* in Dutch), an inexpensive and efficient means of protecting livestock feed from the elements. They were most often built with four poles that were about twenty-feet high, though earlier ones went much higher and had as many as eight posts. By using a jack, the roof could be moved up and down depending on the quantity of hay to be protected. To reduce its weight, the roof was built of light spars and thatch.

The barn, with regard to its situation, size, convenience, and good furnishing is an object, in the mind of a farmer, superior even to that of his dwelling. . . Many don't care how they are lodged, provided that they have a good barn and barnyard, and indeed it is the criterion by which I always judge of a farmer's prosperity. On this building he never begrudges his money. . . . Many farmers have several barracks in their barn-yards where they put their superfluous hay and straw. —J. Hector St. John de Crevecoeur, Orange County, NY, 1782 [*Sketches*, pp. 312–3]

Voorlezer's House

Historic Richmond Town, Staten Island, New York
City of New York and the Staten Island Historical Society,
Staten Island, New York

A *voorlezer*, literally "singing master," assisted the Dutch minister (or dominie) not only in leading the congregation in singing but often as a teacher of their children. The Voorlezer's House on Staten Island, given its unusual full two-story height, apparently served as his home and as a school and meeting place. The house remained that for only five years after which there was a long succession of owners and much modification of its original institutional layout to suit residential and commercial needs.

WINDOW

Based on surviving evidence in the house and a few surviving examples, this leaded casement window is a restored *kloosterkozyn*, having a fixed leaded glass light for the upper transom window and hinged shutter and casement in the lower window. Other types of casements had various combinations of shutters and fixed or hinged glass. The purpose, however, was consistent: to supply daylight from at least one opening, and fresh air or more light from other openings with the option of closing shutters to ward off the heat of summer and the cold of winter. It was not until the nineteenth century when houses were better heated that shutters became "blinds," that is, louvered to exclude direct sunlight but allow ambient light and fresh air to enter.

FRONT

Each floor of the Voorlezer's house has a main room and a smaller rear room; the larger front rooms have gable-end Dutch fireplaces and the lower rear room has a corner fireplace. The second-floor rooms are even higher than the first and the front one has a plastered ceiling, both features bespeaking special use. During the restoration of this museum, evidence for the fireplaces, casement windows, pentice, and extended eaves were found and restored.

The Joseph Guyon House

Historic Richmond Town, Staten Island, New York
City of New York and the Staten Island Historical Society,
Staten Island, New York

Joseph Guyon built this house in about 1740 on his farm on Old Mill Road, Staten Island. Apparently it was an addition to a smaller house that was later removed. He completed the center hall and the room and a half to its left, that was attached to the older wing. Perhaps because he was a bachelor he had no need for the rest of the house. And so it remained when his nephew of the same name inherited the farm. It was not until around 1790, after his death, that the unfinished rooms were completed and a decade or more later bedrooms above this were added. In about 1820 the newer kitchen wing was built, probably replacing the old wing that was removed. Not until the 1840s were nearly all spaces in the house made habitable. The house was moved to Historic Richmond Town in 1962 and is now a museum.

KITCHEN WING

Extended eaves shade and protect the south-facing entrance to both sections of Guyon's house, the walls being of weatherboards except for the three more exposed sides of the main section which are shingled. In the nineteenth century posts were added to the main house eaves, creating a porch effect.

PARLOR

Joseph Guyon's parlor, circa 1740, is a progressive adaptation of the Anglo-Dutch style. A tile-lined jambed fireplace is unified into the room by wall paneling within which a cupboard is set for storage and display. The room is furnished with objects also derived from England except for a Dutch *duffpot* on the hearth which was where embers were stored overnight to be used the next day to light the fire. The smaller room in back contains a fireplace, which suggests it was a bedroom; its front corner location allowed the chimney to exit high on the gambrel roof as does the parlor chimney.

SHUTTER DOG

Even in small details the Dutch added aesthetic appeal to functional objects, hence the graceful S shape of this shutter dog, one of many whimsical designs found on early houses.

The Cornelis Cowenhoven House

Holmdel, Monmouth County, New Jersey

This house, more than others in the region, shows evidence of the earliest type of Dutch structure: two rooms, a steep pitch roof (with no projecting eaves), gable-end Dutch fireplaces, and massive ceiling beams. It also shows many of the changes desired by the mid-eighteenth century: increased depth for more rooms, English fireplaces, and a kitchen wing.

The house has had few owners, no doubt because they have cherished the visual appeal of this early home and as a consequence, have preserved it. It still stands among the fields first cultivated by the Cowenhovens three centuries ago, an increasing rarity in a state so suburbanized.

LATCH HANDLE

Iron work associated with Dutch houses is usually distinctive in design and sometimes in decoration. This thumbpress latch handle is both dated (1752) and stamped **B** in three places, more as decoration (being also backward and upside down) than just the document of a proud maker.

GABLE ENDS

The kitchen wing dates from the mid- to late eighteenth century. When the early windows on the front of the main house were changed in the nineteenth century one of them was moved to the back of the kitchen wing, perhaps saved out of sentiment as it was already heavily weathered. That distress, plus the weathered appearance of original siding shingles, bears witness to the importance of extended eaves in protecting other houses. On the Hendrickson house (p. 215) original siding features are still in excellent condition where protected by extended eaves.

PARLOR

This room originally had a Dutch fireplace in the gable end wall just to the right of the succeeding corner fireplace. When rooms were added to the rear in the mid-eighteenth century, the rear roof was extended at a gentler angle to cover them; the ridge of the roof remained in place. This corner fireplace was then installed in the front right room, suitably positioned to both face into the room, yet exit its chimney through the ridge of the roof. At the same time, an elaborate English-style cupboard was placed in the front corner. These alterations in the mid- to late eighteenth century coincided with a wing being added to the right of the house, likely as a new kitchen; it included a corner cupboard similar to the one shown here.

STAIRWAY

This tightly wound stairway accesses the garret. Beyond the main room, which was likely used for dining, and can be seen from the kitchen through a series of paneled doors. The front door to the main room is split in the Dutch manner. In addition, a two-paneled door provides entry into what was likely the great room or parlor. The original two-paneled door was decoratively painted (*right*).

PAINTED DOOR

The interior door between the two main rooms of the house was decoratively painted with a scene of a grand Netherlandish estate and a vase of flowers, likely by Daniel Hendrickson (1723–88) who married the daughter of the house in 1743. Hendrickson's family, like most others to first settle in Monmouth County, New Jersey, came from Long Island. His personal industry was extraordinary, extending to farming, milling, manufacturing, distilling, shipping, and more. His journals and surviving paintings document a folk talent for portrait and decorative painting. He was so active in the Dutch church that they called him "Dominie Daniel." The use of decorative paint in houses is still evident in The Netherlands but almost entirely painted over in the United States; Hendrickson's decorative house painting is an example of what little survives.

Photo: Courtesy of Mary and Scott Stevenson. The door is now in the permanent collection of the American Folk Art Museum, New York.

The Holmes–Hendrickson House

Holmdel, Monmouth County, New Jersey
Monmouth County Historical Society, Freehold, New Jersey

The main section of this house dates from the mid-eighteenth century, about the time the farm was sold by
Jonathan Holmes to his son William in 1752. The house
itself shows a transition of cultures. The structure and basic
form relates to earlier Dutch houses, but the fireplaces and
decorative details are English.

Like Dutch houses, it has two front rooms and no center
hall. A single front door enters the right parlor directly; the
rear door enters the center of three small half-size rooms at
the back of the house, in effect, a hallway that gives access to
other rooms and to the garret by an enclosed stairway. The
plan is common to many houses in the Dutch areas of New
Jersey and Long Island where earlier two-room houses were
usually expanded a half room deeper.

FRONT

Influenced by the Swedes on
the Delaware River, the Dutch
in this region of New Jersey
also had corner fireplaces
which could be built back-to-
back to heat front and rear
rooms, while exiting smoke
through one flue directly to
the top of the roof at the
gable ends.

FRONT STOOP

One likely function of extended eaves is shown here by the shadow it casts over windows on a summer day, thus reducing the amount of radiant heat entering the house at midday. On winter days the sun is lower in the sky and more welcome warmth can then enter the house. The same eaves also protect the walls and vulnerable windows, shutters, doors, and stoop from as much snow and rain as they would otherwise suffer; this, in turn, prolonged their life spans.

FRONT DOOR

Before the advent of the center hall, entry doors went into the main rooms of a house. In time the convenience of such access was less important than regulating temperature and privacy, which the center hall allowed. In the Hendrickson house the back door could accomplish these goals if the front door, seen here in the living room, was reserved for special occasions.

KAS AND BED

Four post (or tester) beds were common and valued furnishings in most rooms in a Dutch house. In an era before garrets became bedrooms, the family slept in both kitchen and parlor. Curtains provided privacy but also some self-contained winter warmth as the hearth fire chilled through the night. Check fabrics were mentioned in inventories as were the Dutch *kases*. The Dutch preferred this all-purpose storage piece over the English chest of drawers.

Longstreet Farm

Holmdel, Monmouth County, New Jersey
Monmouth County Park System

Longstreet Farm is one of the best preserved Dutch farms thanks to caring generations of owners and the Monmouth County Park System which operates it as a museum. The Dutch barn has been dated by dendrochronology (tree ring dating) to 1792, just before Hendrick Longstreet acquired the farm from his grandfather Hendrick Hendrickson, whose family settled in this region in the 1690s. At this site the visitor has the chance to see many of the structures which once made up the complex of a Dutch farm (p. 174).

CORN CRIB

Corn was a major staple of Dutch diets. Well-aerated corn cribs were best for drying corn so that it could be preserved and later ground to a meal and fed to cattle, pigs, and chickens. But corn's principal use was for *sappaan*, a staple porridge similar to present-day hominy grits. Of this, traveler Peter Kalm remarked: *"There was the same perpetual evening meal of porridge made of corn meal. It was put into a good sized dish and a large hole made in its center into which the milk was poured, and then one proceeded to help oneself."* [*Travels*, p. 629]

This large double-bin corn crib was actually constructed of two mid-nineteenth-century cribs joined by what appear to be Dutch-type through tenons projecting out of the sides, although in fact the joinery is not the same as anchor beams in a Dutch barn. Corn cribs were indispensable because they preserved grain longer than any other type of storage space.

You will remember this particular structure. Some people are, and all should be, furnished with electrical rods. The best way to place them, in order to save expense, is on a high cedar mast situated between the house and the barn. Its power will attract the lightening sufficiently to save both. Mine is so. I once saw its happy effects and blessed the inventor. My barn was then completely full. I valued it at about seven hundred pounds. What should I have done, had not the good Benjamin Franklin thought of this astonishing invention? —J. Hector St. John de Crevecoeur, Orange County, NY, 1782 [*Sketches*, p. 314]

The Hoagland–Durling Barn

Belle Mead, Somerset County, New Jersey

This property stayed in the Hoagland family until acquired by the Wyckoffs in the 1850s. The main section of the house and the barn date from the early nineteenth century.

GABLE

This barn stores bailed hay; with an added side aisle, it can store vehicles as well.

NAVE FLOOR (PEGGED)

Oak floors, inches thick and
tightly pegged, still hold up
the heaviest of machinery
although designed only for
wagons. Timbers up to two-
feet thick and over forty-feet
long were hewn, joined, and
erected by men without
anything but the most
rudimentary contrivances,
a remarkable feat of ingenuity
and neighborly cooperation.

INTERIOR

Machines stilled by changing
economies and generations are
neglected witnesses to the last
uses of Dutch barns. In an era
of suburban development and
silo farming, Dutch barns have
run out of ways to function
and most are succumbing to
disuse and abuse. For want of
a tight roof, these cathedrals
of the countryside are disappearing rapidly, less than six
hundred surviving.

The Roeloff Westervelt House

Tenafly, Bergen County, New Jersey

Roeloff Westervelt (1723–1800) married Dirkjin Taelman in 1745 and built a small one-room house about that time in Tenafly. The original house became the kitchen wing when his grandson Daniel (1779–1877, married 1801) built the main gambrel-roof section of the house in around 1798. Daniel's son Peter added the other wing in 1825. It is hard to imagine a family residing in the small original one-room house for two generations without constructing another house on the site.

GABLE END (EXTERIOR)

The utility of extended eaves is no better demonstrated than in this house. The front and back walls, windows, and doors of the main section have been so well protected from weathering that after two centuries they are in near perfect condition. Winter sun can easily enter the windows, bringing radiant heat to the interior while in summer the eaves shield the windows from much of the higher sun during the heat of the day. A brick bake oven extends out the back of the Dutch fireplace (sheltered by a small roof) on this kitchen wing, the oldest section of the house. The main house's gambrel roof is a conservative holdover of an earlier style—common in this county—its Federal period evidenced by the semi-circular garret window.

DINING ROOM

Despite the up-to-date Federal features of the dining room, the main section of the house, built in 1798, retains evidence (eyelets in the ceiling) of what appear to be curtained bed alcoves in each of the four rooms on the first floor, a much older Dutch practice.

The Federal mantle is carved in a design found throughout the Dutch region; the built-in cupboard, a holdover from the Anglo-Dutch paneled-wall style.

KITCHEN GARRET

The 1745 kitchen wing retains an early or original hood chimney above the unaltered Dutch fireplace (p. 34). Also early or original is an open ladder-like stair to the garret. Evidence of long use and heavy wear on the treads and where the ladder leans against the transverse beam lend credence to the family tradition that the garret was sleeping quarters for the slaves. A trap door now seals off the kitchen limiting the heat that escapes to the garret.

The Jan Zabrieskie House (Steuben House)

North Hackensack, Bergen County, New Jersey
County of Bergen and the Bergen County Historical Society,
River Edge, New Jersey

When Albrecht Zaborowsky came to Old Hackensack, New Jersey (now Ridgefield Park) from Poland in 1662, he founded a dynasty of Bergen County "Zabriskies." In 1745 a descendant, Jan, and his wife Annetje (Ackerman) Zabriskie acquired from Johannes Ackerman a mill and farm. In 1752 they built part of the present house containing a center hall with room on either side, and a pitch roof.

Confiscated from Loyalist Jan Zabriskie in 1781, the state of New Jersey presented the use (and later the title) of the dwelling, gristmill, and about forty acres to Major-General Baron von Steuben, Inspector-General of the Continental Army, on December 23, 1783 in honor of his service to the American cause. He made improvements but because of financial problems, sold it in 1788 to Jan Zabriskie, Jr., son of the builder. It was symbolic of the reconciliation of former adversaries so needed to build and strengthen the young and experimental government.

Dutch houses have survived because they have proved remarkably adaptable to the personal and social needs of each generation. A Dutch ancestor returning today would feel comfortably at home in his old house; most features and furnishings would still be familiar. Conversely, we visualize the past more accurately from historic houses than any other source and live comfortably within them. In this house all the furnishings are antique, yet few would hesitate to "be at home" for a night—or a lifetime.

GABLE (SOUTH)

Prosperity and the need for more room resulted in one or two wings being added to many houses. In this house a radical change occurred, still not clearly understood: two levels of small rear rooms were added, the roof was expanded in gambrel form, a room was added to the north, and bedrooms were created in the garret.

DINING ROOM

Old houses rarely remained frozen in time since they responded to family needs, both physical and social. Houses like the Zabrieskies' expanded to accommodate larger families and were restyled to express changes in personal wealth and family status. With or without changes in architecture, a family could alter their style of living merely by changing furnishings. This usually happened first in the more pubic rooms such as the early-nineteenth-century furniture in the Zabrieskie dining room, reflecting the priority of social rather than functional needs.

KEEPING ROOM

The large English-style fireplace provides support for a bedroom fireplace above. Furnished with the implements and garden herbs of a kitchen, the room shares functions, as in most Dutch houses, with other family needs, such as eating, socializing, and sleeping. This room is referred to as a keeping room, while two rooms behind it with fireplaces may have served kitchen functions, as did an "out kitchen," a separate structure no longer extant.

BEDROOM (SOUTH)

The desire for a garret bedroom with a fireplace was an important cause of the metamorphosis of the Dutch house into something bigger and better—in the eyes of progressive families. The Zabrieskies were just that; they altered their house from five to twelve rooms within a generation.

KEEPING ROOM

In the same room as the spacious fireplace (p. 230) are beds and accouterments of domestic industry, a fair expression of the multipurpose uses to which the Dutch put their rooms.

Appendix

Museums with sites illustrated in this book

The Northern Frontier
The Mohawk and Upper Hudson River Valleys

The Bronck Houses
Greene County Historical Society
Route 9W, Coxsackie, NY 12051
518 731-8862

The Mabee Farm
Route 5S, Rotterdam Junction, NY
Schenectady County Historical Society
32 Washington Avenue, Schenectady, NY 12305
518 374-0263

Palatine Lutheran Church
Old Mill Road (off Route 5), Nelliston, NY 13410
518 993-3539

The Luykas Van Alen House
Route 9, 1 miles south of Kinderhook
Columbia County Historical Society
4 Albany Avenue, Kinderhook, NY 12106
518 758-9265

The Hudson Highlands
Ulster, Dutchess, Westchester, Orange, and Rockland Counties

The Daniel De Klerck House/John DeWint House
Grand Lodge of Free & Accepted Masons (NYS)
20 Livingston Avenue, Tappan, NY 10983
845 359-1359

Gomez Mill House
11 Mill House Road, Marlboro, NY 12542
845 236-3126

Jean Hasbrouck and Abraham Hasbrouck Houses
Huguenot Historical Society/Huguenot Street
18 Broadhead Ave., PO Box 339, New Paltz, NY 12561
845 255-1660

Verplanck-Van Wyck Barn
Mount Gulian Historic Site
145 Sterling Street, Beacon, NY 12508
845 831-8172

Philipsburg Manor
Route 9, North Tarrytown, NY
Historic Hudson Valley, Inc.
150 White Plains Road, Tarrytown, NY 10591
914 631-8200

The Islands and the Jerseys
Long Island, Staten Island, and New Jersey

Holmes-Hendrickson House
Longstreet Road, Holmdel, NJ
Monmouth County Historical Association
70 Court Street, Freehold, NJ 07733
732 462-1466

Monmouth County Park System/Longstreet Farm
Roberts and Holmdel Roads, Holmdel Park
Holmdel, NJ 07733
908 946-3758

New York City Department of Parks and Recreation
Queens County Farm Museum
73-50 Little Neck Parkway, Floral Park, NY 11004
718 347-3276

Minne Schenck House
Old Bethpage Village Restoration
Round Swamp Road, Old Bethpage, NY 11804
516 420-5281

Voorlezer's House and Joseph Guyon House
Staten Island Historical Society
441 Clarke Avenue, Staten Island, NY 10306
718 351-1617

Pieter Claessen Wyckoff House
5902 Canarsie Lane, Brooklyn, NY
Wyckoff House & Association Inc.
PO Box 100-376, Brooklyn, NY 11210
718 629-5400

Jan Zabrieskie House (Steuben House)
North Hackensack, NJ
Bergen County Historical Society
1201 Main Street, River Edge, NJ 07661
201 343-9492

Additional restorations open to the public
John Bowne House, Flushing, NY
Teller or Madam Catharyna Brett Homestead, Beacon, NY
Brooklyn Museum, Brooklyn, NY
Historic New Bridge Landing, River Edge, NJ
Historic Richmond Town, Staten Island, NY
Hurley Historical District, Hurley, NY
Kingston Historic Stockade, Kingston, NY
Frederick Van Cortlandt House, Van Cortlandt Park, Bronx, NY

Bibliography

Primary Sources

Anonymous, "Description of the City of Albany—with a Plate." *Columbia Magazine* (New York), December 1789.

Bullivant, Dr. Benjamin. "A Glance at New York in 1697, The Travel Diary of Dr. Benjamin Bullivant." Edited by Wayne Andrews. *The New-York Historical Society Quarterly*, 60 (1956): pp. 55–73.

Danckaerts, Jasper. *Journal of Jasper Danckaerts, 1678–80.* Edited by Burleigh J. Bartlett and J. Franklin Jameson. New York: Charles Scribner's Sons, 1913.

de Chastellux, Marquis. *Travels in North America in the Years 1780, 1781 and 1782.* Rev. ed., translated by Howard C. Rice, Jr. Chapel Hill: University of North Carolina Press, 1963.
De Crevecoeur, J. Hector St. John. *Letters from an American Farmer.* New York: Penguin Classics, 1986.

_____. *Sketches of Eighteenth-Century America.* New York: Penguin Classics, 1986.

Fontaine, Rev. James. "Journal" (1710–18). In *Memoirs of a Huguenot Family: Translated and compiled from the Original Autobiography of the Rev. James Fontaine.* Translated and edited by Ann Maury, Baltimore: Genealogical Publishing Co., 1967.

Grant, Mrs. Anne. *Memoirs of an American Lady.* Edited by James Grant Wilson. New York: Dodd, Mead and Co., 1909.

Hamilton, Alexander. *Hamilton's Itinerarium...1744.* Edited by Albert Bushnell Hart. St. Louis: privately printed by William K. Bixby, 1907.

Johnson, Warren. *Journal* in *The Papers of Sir William Johnson,* Vol. 13, pp 192–201. Albany: University of the State of New York, 1921–65.

Kalm, Peter. *Peter Kalm's Travels in North America.* Edited by Adolph B. Benson, 2 volumes. Reprint. New York: Dover Publications, 1964.

Knight, Madame Sarah. *The Private Journal Kept by Madame Knight, on a Journey from Boston to New-York, in the Year 1704.* Upper Saddle River, New Jersey: Literature House/Gregg Press, 1970.

Lott, Abraham. "Journal of Voyage on the Hudson and Visit to Kinderhook [1774]." *The Historical Magazine and Notes and Queries Concerning the Antiquities, History and Biography of America.,* Vol. VII, 2nd ser., August 1870.

Strickland, William. *Journal of a Tour in the United States of America, 1794–95.* New York: The New-York Historical Society, 1971.

Van Laer, Arnold J. F., ed. and trans. *Correspondence of Jeremias van Rensselaer 1651–1674.* Albany: University of the State of New York, 1932.

Secondary Sources

Bailey, Rosalie Fellows. *Pre-Revolutionary Dutch Houses and Families in Northern New Jersey and Southern New York.* New York: William Morrow & Company, for the Holland Society of New York, 1936.

Blackburn, Roderic H. and Nancy Kelley (eds). *Dutch Arts and Culture in Colonial America, Proceedings of the Symposium (of the same title, August 1986).* Albany: The Albany Institute of History and Art, 1987.

Blackburn, Roderic H. and Ruth Piwonka. *Remembrance of Patria: Dutch Arts and Culture in Colonial America, 1609–1776.* The Publishing Center for Cultural Resources for The Albany Institute of History and Art, 1988.

Cohen, David Steven. *The Dutch-American Farm.* New York: New York University Press, 1992.

Fitchen, John. *The New World Dutch Barn, A Study of Its Characteristics, Its Structural System, and Its Probable Erection Procedure.* Syracuse University Press. 1968 (Second edition 2001, edited with new material by Gregory D. Huber).

Kammen, Michael. *Colonial New York: A History.* Millwood, New York: KTO Press, 1978.

Meeske, Harrison. *The Hudson Valley Dutch and Their Houses.* Fleischmanns, NY: Purple Mountain Press, 1999 (revised 2001).

Reynolds, Helen Wilkinson. *Dutch Houses in the Hudson Valley before 1776.* New York: Payson and Clarke, for the Holland Society of New York, 1929.

Waterman, Thomas. *The Dwellings of Colonial America.* Chapel Hill: The University of North Carolina Press, 1950.

Further recommended books

Singleton, Esther. *Dutch New York.* New York: Dodd, Mead and Company, 1909.

Singleton, Esther. *Social New York Under the Georges 1714–1776.* New York: D. Appleton and Company, 1902.

Acknowledgments

The text for this book draws on over thirty years spent learning about Dutch houses in Connecticut, Delaware, Massachusetts, the Netherlands, New Jersey, New York, and South Carolina. Countless owners, both private and public, have directly and indirectly informed my knowledge of these houses and other outbuildings. I am especially indebted to the following colleagues in the Netherlands who have shared with me their insights into Dutch architecture and Dutch life: Hank J. Zantkuyl, the long-time head of restoration of buildings for Amsterdam, and Jaap Schipper, the architect in charge of the restoration of Zaanse Schans museum village, among other credits. Both imparted a world of invaluable wisdom to me, especially enlightening me about how human uses of the home help explain house evolution.

I have benefitted from the kind review of the manuscript by colleagues and friends, Ruth Piwonka, Hudson Valley historian and long-time collaborator on similar publications; Dr. David Voorhees, New York historian and editor of *de Halve Maen*, the journal of the Holland Society; Hank Meeske, my partner in unraveling the mysteries of these early houses; Rosemary and John Burgher, friends and diligent restorers of their great early Anglo-Dutch house; and Dr. Anita Schorsch, an enthusiastic and perceptive convert to the sensibilities of Dutch culture. I have also made good use of Dr. Firth Fabend's thoughtful analysis of the Dutch. A number of friends and colleagues with expertise on Dutch and Georgian houses have shared their ideas and suggestions for which I am most grateful: William Palmer, an architect whose expertise in preservation issues is most valued; Donald Carpentier, creator of Eastfield Village, who has loaned objects for photographs and shared insights into the many houses and other structures he has found, studied, or moved; William McMillan, supervisor of restoration for Historic Richmond Town, Staten Island, who has made helpful comments especially on house types and features in his region; and Tim Adriance for his perceptive understanding of Dutch houses, especially those of Bergen County, New Jersey. Their contributions to the improvement of my thoughts and writing is most appreciated.

I wish to make special mention of my collaborator, Geoffrey Gross, whose talents, energy, and disposition are truly exceptional. He is a master of fine photography. I have seen him take a whole day for one shot (through dozens of exposures), using six lights to create an image that looks convincingly like natural lighting. It takes all that to perfect sunlight. If you see in these images a reflection of Vermeer's haunting interiors it is no accident. Geoffrey sees light on surfaces in the same way old master painters did, and he can evoke those qualities on film.

My last thoughts are for those who have preceded us in the endeavor to understand the Dutch and their houses. I made extensive use of the following sources in this book and wish to extend my gratitude to these authors for their contribution to Dutch studies: Helen Wilkinson Reynolds, *Dutch Houses in the Hudson Valley before 1776*;

Rosalie Fellows Bailey, *Pre-Revolutionary Dutch Houses and Families in Northern New Jersey and Southern New York*; Dr. David Steven Cohen, *The Dutch-American Farm*; Harrison Meeske, *The Hudson Valley Dutch and Their Houses*, who also kindly contributed the foreword to this volume; John Fitchen, *The New World Dutch Barn*; the publications of Gregory Huber; the journals of members of the Dutch Barn Preservation Society and the Society for the Preservation of the Hudson Valley Vernacular Architecture (especially Peter Sinclair of the latter); Thomas Waterman, *The Dwellings of Colonial America.*

—*Roderic H. Blackburn*

The original idea for this project came from Tim Adriance of Bergen County, New Jersey. His enthusiasm for Dutch-American history and invaluable help provided the initial impetus to begin. Shirley Dunn's and Allison Bennett's book *Dutch Architecture Near Albany: The Polgreen Photographs* ignited the spark that continues to drive me.

To the many homeowners, historic site workers, historians, and aficionados of old houses I can only reiterate my deepest appreciation for the time you spent with me and the information you shared. This is particularly true of the many who, often without notice or introduction, opened up their homes to me, in true colonial Dutch-American fashion. The warmth and kindness shown to me while my photography equipment littered your kitchens, living rooms, and bedrooms is without bounds.

From the very beginning, my colleagues Tim Campbell and Dane Shitagi were available and willing to provide whatever photographic guidance was required, often at a moment's notice. Charles Gehring and staff at the New Netherland Project have, and continue to be, valuable and friendly sources of information not available anywhere else. The members of the Dutch Barn Preservation Society have been very helpful and responsive. The encouragement offered by David Vietor has been most welcome. Reverend Zabriskie and Dr. Canfield of Rutgers University have also provided encouragement.

The enthusiasm of David Morton at Rizzoli has been extremely beneficial. This book would not be possible without the editing and organizational skills of Kristen Schilo. Her patience with me and my inability to adhere to deadlines was endless. The layout and design of this book exceeds my grandest expectation. The synergistic effect of my photographs is the result of Abigail Sturges with the assistance of Sarah Bryant. Her careful handling of these images completes the statements I attempted to make.

I would like to express my appreciation to Elaine Hayes, executive director, and Denise Schirmer, program associate, of Mount Gulian Historic Site for inviting me to show these photographs and for all their help and assistance in coordinating the exhibit. Wray and Loni Rominger of Purple Mountain Press have proved instrumental in boosting me and my work.

As the prime force for this book, I wish to convey my deepest appreciation to all those who gave freely of their time and knowledge on the subject of the colonial Dutch and their culture. I am especially indebted to the homeowners and museum and site managers who graciously indulged me in my quest to fully experience, through photography, all aspects of this culture. It is through this non-verbal visual experience that I present a view of what would grow into our contemporary American society and culture.

Without the help, encouragement, and guidance of my very good friend Les Morsillo, this project would have ended before it started. More than anyone else, he has always been supportive of me and my work, as has my longtime friend and college roommate, Thomas Carr. Both these friends have been there for me when all others have fled. I also wish to thank my daughter Alice Tobin-Gross for providing the artwork for the exhibition announcement. Then seven years old, she was able to spot and identify gambrel roofs, and became an expert on all historic site "gift shoppes" between Manhattan and Albany.

Special thanks to Greg Huber who unselfishly made available to me his many years of extensive field work and knowledge of early Dutch-American architecture. I refer the interested reader to his timely contributions to the recently republished *The New World Dutch Barn* by John Fitchen.

Another special thank you to Harrison Meeske whose recent book *The Hudson Valley Dutch and Their Houses* provided me with an easy path. His ideas and suggestions gave me the background necessary to discover Dutch architecture. To Roderic Blackburn; seldom have I received the encouragement I got from you. I greatly appreciate the help of Susan Piatt. I am looking forward to the next time I hear you say, "Hey Geoffrey, let's do a book!"

Without the active assistance and encouragement of Dr. David William Voorhees, Annette van Rooy, Walton Van Winkle III, and Dora Koutelas of The Holland Society, this project would not have been possible.

A very special thank you to Mrs. Anna Glen Vietor. Her unfailing support for this project enhanced the overall quality and thoroughness of my photographs. Rolland A. Miner of the New World *Dutch Barn Survey 2000*, provided essential background information.

Many others have contributed materially to this book, either in person or by influence of their own work. I list each here with great appreciation: Richard Anderson; Arnie Color Lab; Aurora Color; Richard Babcock; Willis Barshied; Mike Barbieri; Logan Blackburn;

John Bonafide; Jack Braunlein; Ursula C. Brecknell; Barbara Brinkley; Ann Brookmeyer; Mike Cohen; Samuel Chamberlain; William Congdon; Page Ayres Cowley; Keith Cramer; Joan Davidson; Margaret de Mott Brown; Antoinette Davis; Steve Estimiades; Wanda Fleck; H. L. Funk; Mike Gladstone; Charles Glassner of JenkinsTown Antiques; Bob Griffin; Scott Hafner; The Honorable Robert Heinsch; Scot Heyl; Nick Howe; Gail Hunton; Marty Hylton; Sara Jarkow; Emil Johnson; Philip Katz; Karen Kihlstrom; Simon Lee; Leslie LeFavre; Steve Levine; Simon Lewis; Chester Ludlow; Rita Maas; Shelby Mattice; Susan McClellan; Richard Mills; David and Trina Osher; Sharon Palmer; T. H. Prudon; Chris Ricciardi; Mary Rupert; Liz Saplin; Alvin Shiffer; Peter Sinclair; Nancy Sirkis; Paul and Mary Spencer; Kevin Stayton; Steve Swift; Lilly Tallapassee; TSI Color; Tommy Twang and Yukon Cornelius; John Van Schaick; David Vietor; Mr. and Mrs. C. D. Ward; Brad Whipple; Prof. A.J. Williams-Myers; Greg Wilson; Ellen Wolk; Donna Wolf; Kevin Wright; June Zaidain; and Nancy Ziegler.

Dr. Lee Ellen Griffith, director, and Bernadette Rogoff, museum curator, the Monmouth County Historical Association; McKelden Smith and Burns Patterson, Historic Hudson Valley; Gail Youngelson, Peter Curtis, Carol Hagglund, Mary Ann Hunting, and Steve Kozak, Philipsburg Manor; Stacy C. Hollander, senior curator and director of exhibitions, The American Folk Art Musem; James McKenna, Old Bethpage Village; William Maurer, director, and Ellen Healy, curator, the Gomez Mill House; Amy Fishetti, director, the Queens County Farm Museum; and William McMillan, Richmondtown Restoration.

We jointly wish to express special thanks to the private owners of sites (or objects) who have graciously accepted our invitation to be included in this book: Willis Barshied; Anne Bienstock; DeGuerre and Roderic Blackburn; Rosemary and John Burgher; Donald Carpentier; Harriet Durling; Randall Evens and Carey Feder; James Joseph and Gary Tinterow; Tom Lanni; Peggy Lampman and Ian Nitschke; Carolina and Livio Lazzari; Glen and Joan O'Neill; Iris and Jonathan Oseas; Brian Parker; Carol Parks; Stacy and Robert Schmeterer; Mary and Scott Stevenson; Donald Teidman; Carl Toughey; Page and Jonathan Trace; and Kevin and Janet Trimble. Also William and Jean Appeal; Harriet Durling; Harold B. Jones; Silvia and Paul Lawlor; and Kenneth Snyder.

The participating historical societies and museums include: Bergen County Historical Society; Columbia County Historical Society; Grand Lodge of Free & Accepted Masons (NYS); Greene County Historical Society; Hendrick I. Lott House Preservation Association, Inc.; Huguenot Historical Society/Huguenot Street; Mount Gulian Historic Site; New York City Department of Parks and Recreation; Old Bethpage Village Restoration; Schenectady County Historical Society; Staten Island Historical Society; and Wyckoff House & Association Inc.

The photo of the painted door for the Cornelis Cowenhoven House; courtesy of Mary and Scott Stevenson. This door is now part of the permanent collection of the The American Folk Art Museum. The public sites which are part of this book are listed in the appendix for the convenience of readers who would like to visit them. These house museums, and the staff members, have been most helpful in giving us access to their buildings and grounds. To all of them we extend our warm thanks.

—*Geoffrey Gross*

Index

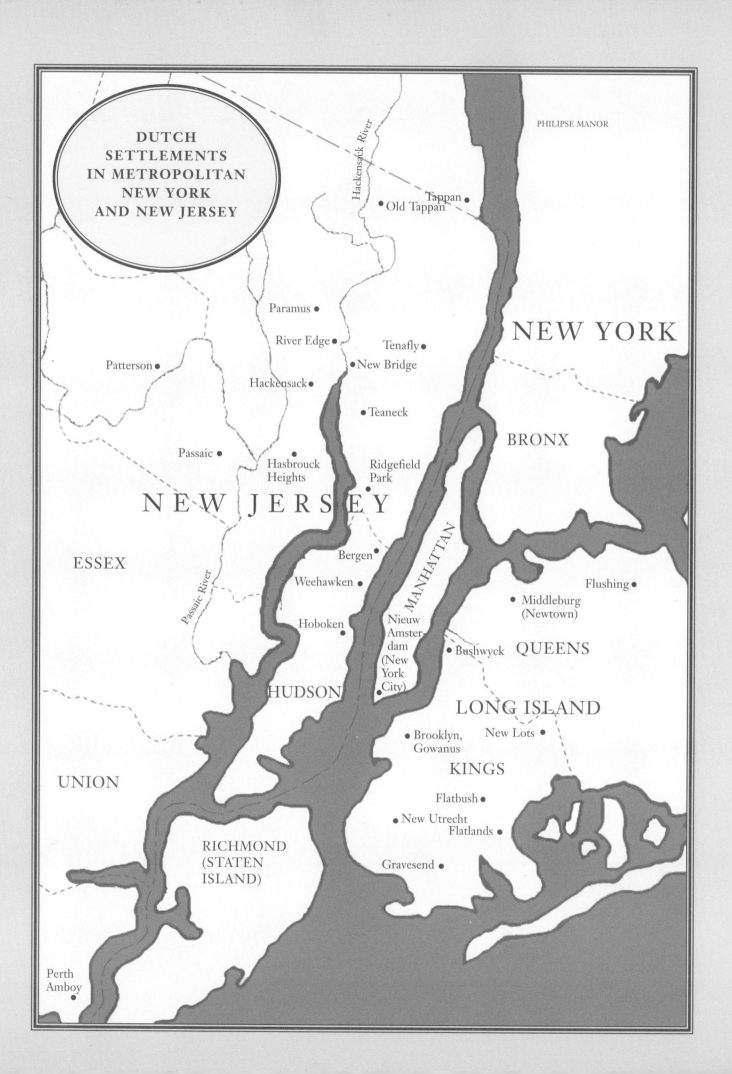